THE
DESKTOP
Guide
TO
DESKTOP
Publishing

JOHN WALKER

ISBN 1-85181-164-8

Published by:
Glentop Press Ltd
Standfast House
Bath Place
Barnet
Herts EN5 5XE
Tel: 01–441 4130

Trademarks
PostScript is a trademark of Adobe Systems. Stop Press is a trademark of Advanced Memory Systems. PageMaker is a trademark of Aldus Corporation. LaserWriter and Macintosh are trademarks licensed to Apple Computer, Inc. Amiga is a trademark of Commodore/Amiga Inc. CP/M, GEM, GEM Draw, GEM Paint, GEM Write are trademarks of Digital Research Inc. PageSetter and LaserScript PageSetter are trademarks of Gold Disk Inc. Fleet Street Editor and Fleet Street Publisher are trademarks of Mirrorsoft Ltd. Ventura Publisher is a trademark of Rank Xerox Ltd. There are a great many products mentioned in the course of this book. Please note that, unless otherwise stated, they are all trademarks and protected by law.

Contents

Preface

This book is not only about desktop publishing, but it is also an example of it. It was written, typeset, designed and printed on the top of my desk. I used a 512K Commodore Amiga 1000 computer running Gold Disk's *PageSetter* and *PageSetter LaserScript* software.

The illustrations were created in *PageSetter's* graphics editor, using in one instance *Zuma Fonts*, a collection of fonts for dot–matrix printers. The pages were printed on an Apple LaserWriter, which also sat on my desktop.

In truth, programs such as *PageSetter* are intended for producing newsletters rather than books, for they lack fine control over the placing of type. Nevertheless, I hope it demonstrates some of the possibilities of desktop publishing, rather than its limitations.

I owe thanks to many people who helped me during its writing, especially to Pat Bitton, marketing director of Mirrorsoft, who kept me up–to–date with the many versions of *Fleet Street Editor* and *Fleet Street Publisher*, to Edward Goring, for sharing some of his journalistic expertise with me, and to Eddy Maddix, of Glentop Press, for his good advice.

I owe more than gratitude to my wife Barbara for her continuing forbearance and encouragement. And thanks to my son Barnaby for not complaining too much when he wanted to play *Marble Madness!* and I needed to typeset.

John Walker
Bath
July 1987

Introduction

ESKTOP Publishing is one of those ugly, meaningless phrases that computing seems to attract. Who wants to publish desktops, after all? But behind the jargon lies one of the most interesting and exciting of all applications involving microcomputer. Desktop publishing, or DTP for short, is a means of producing with a microcomputer, printed material that can range from books, reports, newsletters, pamphlets, and magazines to mailing shots and comics. Its advantage over conventional printing and publishing is that it is quicker, cheaper and easier.

One person with the right software can perform those tasks that normally take teams of people: designing the layout of the page or pages, setting the type, adding illustrations, pasting it into position and proof-reading it. It is cheaper because less people are involved and the equipment is much less expensive than that used in conventional printing. It is easy enough to be done by virtually anyone, providing that he or she is interested, and not frightened by computers.

The requirements are a computer with a disk drive and the right software, which can cost from pocket-money prices to more than the computer it runs on, depending on the sophistication of the system. The final stage – of printing the publication – requires, naturally enough, a printer of some sort. This can range from a dot-matrix machine sharing the desktop to a laser printer, photo-copier or a traditional printing press.

"Desktop" refers not merely to the fact that computer publishing is done on the top of a desk, but to the metaphor of a desktop containing folders and files, notebooks, pens and pencils that appears on-screen when DTP software is used.

What this book offers is a crash course in the techniques of desktop publishing, from writing the words and drawing the pictures to laying out the result in a pleasing fashion, printing and publishing it. It is intended for the uninitiated or those who are beginning to discover the possibilities of do-it-yourself publishing and wish to find out more. It is for amateurs rather than professionals. Amateur means not only the inexpert but the enthusiastic, and a little time spent with a desktop publishing system will turn anyone involved in the production of printed material into an enthusiast.

The emphasis is on desktop publishing systems that use interactive page layout, programs that mimic the normal methods of making up a page, in which you arrange words and pictures to achieve the result you want. It is this aspect of desktop publishing that gives it its fascination and flexibility. The ability to see exactly what is happening makes page layout programs very suitable for use by those without a specific training in graphic arts. Not only can you see what you are doing, but you can make changes in a moment, shifting a block of text or altering the size of an illustration. You can experiment and check the results immediately.

The advice given, on such matters as typography and design, is applicable to all kinds of desktop publishing, whatever computer or software you use or are thinking of acquiring. It explains the rules and procedures of producing printed matter by the time—honoured conventions, drawing on the experience of the past. But it also explores the unconventional.

I have written the book from the standpoint of one person working with a microcomputer who is responsible for desktop publishing, whether for his or her own pleasure or profit, or as part of a community effort, or as a department within a business. There are, of course, businesses with their own graphic designers, who would be the ideal people to oversee the layout of a publication, and their own public relations departments, who would be responsible for the editing, receiving copy over a network of computers.

Included is information on off—beat typography. I confess to a weakness for the productions of Victorian jobbing printers, who whacked into their posters any combination of typefaces that came to hand. It is the sort of printing that causes professional designers and typographers to come out in a rash. The rules of what was right and what was wrong in typography and make—up grew out of centuries of craft. The great skills of past printers are no longer as necessary as they used to be, and many of their practices, their rules of thumb, are also obsolete.

Thin or spidery typefaces were not part of the repertoire of the average printer, for instance. The reason was a mechanical, rather than an aesthetic, one: thin type cast in metal broke easily or soon became worn, producing blurred print. Thin faces can be produced without problems in desktop publishing. But the impression lingers that such typefaces are somehow "bad".

New technology demands new approaches; it cannot be shackled by the old. With DTP software, you can achieve results in manipulating and rearranging type that would have been virtually impossible or extremely difficult previously. It seems silly not to take advantage of such opportunities, even though the best authorities on print design will tell you it is not done. The great advantage of such software is that it makes "what if" experimentation easy. Only by trying everything will you discover what works for you. Desktop publishing means that the old rule-book has been thrown away – and a new one has yet to be written. The message is: be uninhibited.

One further assumption is made: that you have something you wish to communicate to others, whether you're a corporation seeking to cut costs in printing reports, a publisher of a newsletter, a vicar with a parish magazine, a teacher who wants to create a class magazine, a schoolboy setting up in opposition to *Mad* magazine, a plumber or builder needing to advertise his services or a poet anxious to publish his own work.

Nothing quite like desktop publishing has happened in printing and publishing since that April day in 1455, when an irascible and obscure goldsmith, down on his luck, changed the world. His name was Johann Gutenberg and he did it by perfecting the use of moveable type and so bringing into being the quick and easy duplication of books.

For the first time, writers could reach in a matter of months a vast audience (at least, in comparison with what had gone before). Ideas, theories, opinions, views on society and how it operated were free from former restraints.

As Britain's William Caxton, a manuscript-copyist turned pioneer printer-publisher (and writer) put it in his first printed work, "this book is not written with pen and ink as other books be, to the end that every man may have them at once, for all the books of this story here emprynted as ye see were begun in one day and finished in one day".

This change in the technology of printing is one of those decisive moments in history, perhaps the beginning of the modern world. Before Gutenberg, a man with a library of 80 or so books – such as William Ravenstone who probably taught Geoffrey Chaucer at St Paul's School in the 1350s – was considered a phenomenon. Knowledge was a secondhand process – most had to rely on someone else's explanation of a text and their understanding of it would come from hearing it read aloud.

After Gutenberg, knowledge was easier to acquire. Scholars were able to tap the riches of the past. In the following two centuries, some two million books containing texts of classical writers were published. From those who could read but were not skilled in Latin or Greek came a demand for books in their native tongue, boosting the creation of national, rather than tribal, identity. Nothing was to be the same again.

As Marshall McLuhan put it in his *Understanding Media*, "Typography created a medium in which it was possible to speak out loud and bold to the world itself...Boldness of type created boldness of expression."

The invention of moveable type marked the beginning of the industrial revolution. Printing became the first industry to develop mass production, an approach that swiftly led to specialisation so that the old system of handwritten manuscripts, where students became their own publishers by copying classic texts, gave way to the new, in which individuals were replaced by groups of men each involved only in a particular aspect of the work.

Revolutions begin in unexpected places. Nothing much happened in printing or publishing after Gutenberg's time until 1985 except for mechanical improvements. The increasing specialisation meant that small designer–printer–publishers like Gutenberg disappeared. Type designers were rarely printers, and printers were not often publishers. Power – the ability to control the printed word – became more concentrated, which affected not only the methods of printing, but the content of what was printed. Johann Gutenberg may seem a long time dead. But what happened in his time is happening again.

Desktop publishing, is arguably the single most important use of computers so far. It is certainly the biggest revolution in printing and publishing since he inadvertently ushered in that information explosion whose shockwaves continue to ripple through our civilisation. Apart from cutting printing costs in businesses, desktop publishing brings power to the ordinary people.

It makes it easy for anyone to communicate directly with others without a printer or a publisher standing between him or her and his or her readers. The joy of microcomputers is that it frees us from much of the work involved, making it not only easy, but fun to produce one's own publications.

Desktop publishing has existed for no more than a couple of years. You can date it from the introduction of laser printers for microcomputers in late 1985. At its best, which requires the use of such printers, it can almost equal the quality of conventional print. But the best requires a considerable investment. Yet for a small outlay, covering the cost of an 8–bit computer, a dot–matrix printer and the right software, you can achieve pleasing results – and gain a great deal of enjoyment as well. Who could ask for more?

Despite its recent beginnings, there is already considerable opposition to DTP. I have heard grumbles that all DTP publications "look the same", as if that were not also true of most conventionally printed material. You also hear moans that the design of many DTP publications is abysmal. That may be perfectly true, but it seems beside the point. The standard will improve. At the least, DTP makes more people aware of design, of quality of print, of good and bad typography – and that cannot be a bad thing. After all, the standard of much printed matter, from paperback books to magazines, is low.

The grumbling is natural. It comes from those who feel their livelihoods threatened. But DTP will need talented designers, typographers and graphic artists if it is to reach its full potential. Rather than complaining, they should be busy acquiring a new skill. The reaction to computers was much the same. Just as computer professionals used to explain that their machines were much too difficult for ordinary people to use and understand, so typographers have tended made a mystery of their craft, adding a barely perceptible serif here, removing a slight flourish there – and often forcing upon us a stereotyped monotony.

The result has been typefaces that admirably fulfill two purposes: they are easy to read, and they allow as many words as possible to be crammed upon a page, so saving paper, which is a commodity that grows ever more expensive. Designers, for all their fastidiousness, have helped impose upon us extremely dull–looking books and periodicals. They have banished, for the most part, decoration and illustration from all but expensive coffee–table books.

Elaborate chapter headings have gone, as have fancy initial letters. Printer's flowers, those little decorative shapes that can be formed into beautiful patterns, lie wilting, dusty and forgotten at the back of workshops. They give us books with measly margins, dull title pages and blank end papers. They are all refinement and restraint, for the best of reasons, which are economic.

But their rules do not have to be ours. In his standard history *The Making of Books*, Sean Jennet admits "some of the fun was lost by the printer when the right of design was taken away". Desktop publishing lets us recapture that fun. Like the craftsman–printers of four hundred years ago, we can control the whole process, from designing the typeface to laying out illustrations and text on the page, adding some decorative flourishes, and printing it.

Desktop publishing can fulfill two objectives: it provides creative pleasure, and it enables you to communicate more effectively and cheaply with others. Typographers often feel that their craft is too important a matter to be left to printers. They will explain that they imposed taste on the jobbing printer who, without guidance, "played like a delighted child with crowds of gimcrack faces and fantastic ornaments that descended like gaudy balloons upon him," to quote again from Sean Jennett. I'm all for balloons, circuses and play. What the austere keepers of the tradition forget is that there is an alternative approach to publishing. It is largely forgotten because it was devoted to ephemera, although at various times it has had mass appeal. It is to be found in posters, in the ballads and broadsheets that were sold at street corners and at the foot of gibbets from Elizabethan to Victorian times.

They are examples of vigorous amateur printing. They are primitive. But they have an undeniable charm and liveliness. They were also popular, evidence that professional gloss and beautiful design are not essential to effective communication.

Decoration, said one leading designer recently, is romance. Decoration in printing can be traced back to illuminated manuscripts and forward through William Morris's elaborate books, where text and illustration form one integrated whole, to the psychedelic underground newspapers of the '60s and the punk record album sleeves of today. Desktop publishing gives decoration the chance to make a come-back in print.

Of course, desktop publishing has its limitations. Just as printed books looked tawdry when put against the finest hand-written manuscripts, so the quality of DTP output cannot compare with the best letter-press productions; on the other hand, it stands up very well when put against much conventional run-of-the-press printing. Most of its problems will disappear with time. Remember, desktop publishing is less than three years old and, indeed, has only just reached the IBM PC, the standard business micro. It is still pioneering days.

Anyone can now communicate with an audience without any intervention from others. It requires no long apprenticeship, although an awareness of the disciplines of the art and craft of printing and design will be an asset. There are many books on typography and layout that you may read, but there is nothing to beat the experience of actually producing a publication.

The result may not always satisfy the experts or the purists, the sticklers for correctness and rules, but that is a matter of little importance. Something worth doing is worth doing badly, as well as well. "Damn braces. Bless relaxes," said William Blake, who, of course, was not only an artist and poet, but also the printer and publisher of his own illuminated and illuminating books.

Part One
Words

Chapter 1: Typography

It is an odd thought that the typefaces we use today derive from the handwritten styles perfected by German and Italian scribes, as well as from the work of stone–masons celebrating the glory that was Rome more than 2,000 years ago. Printing was originally regarded as a means of mechanising handwriting, although later it came closer to engraving. Because scribes over the centuries had developed a uniform style of writing, give or take a few quirks of nationality and individuality, early printers tried to imitate the best calligraphy.

1.1 Type classifications

Type can be divided into various groupings. In each group there are different typefaces, often named after the person who designed them, such as Bodoni and Garamond. Each typeface consists of a family, comprising all its different styles: regular, a thinner version of the characters known as light, a heavier version called bold, a smaller one called condensed, a wider one called expanded, a slanting one known as italic and so on. One style and size of type is referred to as a font (or fount) and consists of all the characters in that style: the alphabet from A–Z and a–z, numbers from 0–9 and various punctuation marks and special letters such as the ampersand.

The typefaces used in printing can be divided roughly into six kinds, although the British Standards Institute defines nearly a dozen different groupings.

The four main divisions can be described as:

- Black letter (or Gothic.)
- Roman (or Serif.)
- Slab Serif
- Sans–Serif.

There are two other styles, of lesser importance:

- Cursive, based on informal writing styles.
- Decorative, which is pictorial in style.

1.2 Black letter

Black letter was the first typeface to be set in moveable metal type, due to the fact that Johann Gutenburg, the man usually credited with creating mechanised printing, lived and worked in Mainz. He based his font on the

Times Roman
ABCDEFGHIJKLMNOPQRSTUVWXYZ 1234567890
?!@#$%^&*()_+|[]{}:;"',.<>
abcdefghijklmonoprstuvwxyz

Times Bold
ABCDEFGHIJKLMNOPQRSTUVWXYZ 1234567890
?!@#$%^&*()_+|[]{}:;"',.<>
abcdefghijklmonoprstuvwxyz

Times Italic
ABCDEFGHIJKLMNOPQRSTUVWXYZ 1234567890
?!@#$%^&()_+|[]{}:;"',.<>*
abcdefghijklmonoprstuvwxyz/n

Times Bold Italic
ABCDEFGHIJKLMNOPQRSTUVWXYZ 1234567890
?!@#$%^&*()_+|[]{}:;"',.<>
abcdefghijklmonoprstuvwxyz/n

Helvetica
ABCDEFGHIJKLMNOPQRSTUVWXYZ 1234567890
?!@#$%^&*()_+|[]{}:;"',.<>
abcdefghijklmonoprstuvwxyz

Helvetica Bold
ABCDEFGHIJKLMNOPQRSTUVWXYZ 1234567890
?!@#$%^&*()_+|[]{}:;"',.<>
abcdefghijklmonoprstuvwxyz

Helvetica Oblique
ABCDEFGHIJKLMNOPQRSTUVWXYZ 1234567890
?!@#$%^&()_+|[]{}:;"',.<>*
abcdefghijklmonoprstuvwxyz

Helvetica Bold Oblique
ABCDEFGHIJKLMNOPQRSTUVWXYZ 1234567890
?!@#$%^&*()_+|[]{}:;"',.<>
abcdefghijklmonoprstuvwxyz

Figure 1.1: *Part of two families of type – Helvetica, a sans–serif face, and Times, a serif face – in some of their contrasting styles.*

work of German scribes. It needed more than 300 letter shapes rather than the 26 letters of the alphabet because it imitated a hand–written style which was full of abbreviations, ligatures and other peculiarities of style, but it has never been popular outside Germany and a few other parts of Europe.

It survives in signs for Olde Englishe Tea Shoppes, in the titles of a few olde–fashioned newspapers, in wedding and funereal announcements and some legal documents. It is not easy to read and is suitable only for short messages, to which it lends a somewhat spurious dignity. If you do use it, restrict yourself to upper–and–lower case. If it is set in all capitals it looks awful and is virtually unreadable.

1.3 Roman

The Italians hated black letter, which is why they called it Gothic – another word for barbarian – even though it was the Germans who brought printing to their country. Italian scribes wrote in two styles, one formal and the other informal, which as Roman and Italic remain the most elegant and widely used of typefaces.

What distinguishes the Roman style is the variation in thickness of different parts of the letters, which imitates the act of writing with a pen, and its serifs, those short lines, or brackets, at the end of the stroke of a letter. It was the Roman stone–masons who invented the serif. Try cutting a letter in stone, and you will discover that it seems to require a definite end to its shape, which a serif supplies.

The first Roman type–faces resembled in form the inscriptions on the Trajan column in Rome, which dates from 114 AD and is regarded as the most perfect of all Roman lettering. Appearing in Venice in the late 1400s, they were based on the hand of Italian scribes. They are often referred to as Old Face or Old style and are best exemplified by the type called Garamond.

At the end of the 17th century the French redesigned Roman faces according to a complex mathematical formula. The serifs were not as slanted and the curves were less pronounced. William Caslon and, especially, John Baskerville were the typecutters who introduced the style into Britain and their faces are still in use today.

This style is called Transitional, since it stood between the old and the Modern style, introduced at the end of the eighteenth century. The Modern face was more machine–made in style, with less variation in the thickness of the strokes and straight, rather than curved, serifs. Perhaps the best of them was that cut by an Italian, Giambattista Bodoni, who used thin, horizontal serifs that owed nothing to styles of handwriting. Roman type remains the most elegant and formal of styles. It exudes class. It is ideal for any publication intended to impress. It is also, as the main or body-text, the most readable.

1.4 Slab serif

Slab serif type is made up of much thicker strokes than the Roman. The serifs, as their name suggests, are thick and square rather than curved. Such fonts, which found great popularity among the Victorians, are also known as Egyptian or Mechanistic. They are closer in feeling to sans-serif faces.

1.5 Sans-serif

Letters without a serif – hence sans-serif – can be said to derive from the Greeks, although their popularity is a much more recent development and is the result of the realisation that there is no reason, other than tradition, for metal type to resemble handwriting. Sans-serif letters are usually of the same thickness throughout. They made their appearance in Victorian times, when they seemed symbolic of the machine-age, with their suggestion of force and even brutality.

There are a few sans-serifs which are closer in feel to Roman and owe their inspiration to letters incised in stone. But most sans types are more vulgar than Roman. They shout where the other maintains a genteel drawl. You see them in the headlines of tabloid newspapers, on advertisements and billboards. They convey a sense of urgency, an example of the way the medium can be the message.

Such styles are usually restricted to display types – that is for headlines in a newsletter, magazine or poster – since they can be tiring to read when used in a great deal of text, although they are perfectly acceptable for a piece of writing of less than book-length.

For those using a dot-matrix printer to produce a master copy of a document, sans-serif faces are more acceptable than Roman. One of the problems in using a dot-matrix printer is that large lettering in the Roman style tends to look anything but elegant.

Microcomputers have two failings in creating graphics: they cannot draw circles or curves well, nor straight lines except at an angle of 45, 90, 135, 180, 225 or 270 degrees, that is vertically, horizontally or on the diagonal. As the on-screen picture is made up of a sequence of pixels, or dots, a circle or a line at an angle is stepped, so that the result is an extremely jagged line.

The elegant curve and the swelling and narrowing line of Roman letters is transformed into an angular mess. The result looks anything but refined and

Gothic or Black letter

Roman elegance

Slab Serif or

Egyptian

Sans serif face

Cursive font

Cursive urgency

Decorative face

Figure 1.2: *The six main families of typefaces: Black letter, which is commonly called Gothic; Roman or serif, which is the most legible of types; slab serif, which was beloved by Victorians and can still be effective in advertisements; sans serif, which is a more modern face; cursive, which imitates pen strokes and can suggest formality or haste; and decorative, which is represented here by a font that resembles stencilled lettering.*

it means that other typefaces must be sought if something pleasing is to be achieved. Sans–serif styles, which are far rougher, suffer the loss of elegance much better.

The problem is not an insoluble one, even though a dot–matrix printer usually produces a pixel–by–pixel printout – a graphic dump of what is on the television or monitor screen. It is possible to overcome this, and there is at least one printer driver (for *Publishing Partner* running on an Atari ST) that does produce curves without jagged edges by recalculating in memory the shapes of the letters before they are printed.

Presumably as desktop publishing establishes itself, such drivers will become more common. The results so far do not match laser printers, but they are a great improvement on the quality of other dot–matrix printing.

1.6 Cursive
This describes a range of types that copies the styles of handwriting, from the elegantly formal copperplate to those that resemble letters scribbled in haste. They are of limited use, although a microcomputer linked to a graphics tablet makes it possible to use one's own handwriting in desktop publishing.

1.7 Decorative
Printers usually dub as decorative any style that cannot be easily categorised. It is used here to cover those unusual faces, such as letters made from trees or twigs, which come closer to illustration than to conventional printing. They can play a useful part in desktop publishing, for less formal purposes.

These exotica derive from Victorian printers who were not inhibited by matters of typographical taste, and from the artists of the Judenstil, who created the style known as Art Nouveau and invented typefaces intended to convey emotions or to imitate actions. Their inspiration continued until the 1920s and is also to be seen in the many extraordinary Art Deco typefaces.

Art Deco itself, with its curvilinear and geometric shapes, is a response to the machine–age and possibly closer in feel to the future typefaces that desktop publishing is bound to inspire than the conventional fonts deriving from printing with hot metal. Sobriety returned until the 1960s, when the designers of the newspapers of the underground press created psychedelic effects.

In more recent times, subversive typography surfaced as elaborate graffiti on city walls, and as a punk phenomenon. The group The Sex Pistols were as much to do with fashion and design as music, and were identified by a distinctive style of lettering that resembled a ransom note from a kidnapper, all individual letters that seemed to have been cut from various newspaper headlines and stuck down higgledy–piggledy. What all these have in common is the use of type as an element of decoration as well as of communication.

1.8 Type as decoration

Decoration and ornamentation has almost disappeared from modern printing, which has become ever more functional in its approach to communication. Indeed, the use of fancy borders or unusual typefaces seems to be regarded as a solecism, something grossly improper. As Alison Harding writes in her recent monograph *Ornamental Alphabets and Initials*, "the aesthetic problem of the place of ornamentation in printing has remained unresolved to the present time".

It is clear is that this is an age of puritanism in printing, of the chaste page unsullied by ornamental excess, perhaps as a reaction against the exuberance of the Victorian age. It may well also have much to do with the increasing mechanisation of printing. In its early days, printing was closer to other crafts. The illustrators of illuminated manuscripts used the same pattern books as stone–masons as a guide to decorated letters.

The computer has brought back a more individual approach. The modern equivalent of medieval pattern books is the clip art increasingly being produced for desktop publishing. Of course, many DTP publications – company reports, newsletters, brochures, forms – will follow the plain style of conventional printing of today.

For other publications – flysheets, advertisements, personal letters, community publications – a more personal style is appropriate. As the eminent designer Kenneth Grange pointed out recently the British have become frightened of decoration. Yet people have always added ornamentation and decoration to flat surfaces, and there is no reason why print should be plain. It is easy, after all, in desktop publishing to overlay letters on patterned backgrounds, to create bizarre alphabets, and to use letter shapes creatively.

Restraint is what marks British typography now. But look back and you can find books containing marvellous and intricate ornament that added to the pleasure of reading. Fantastic alphabets created from landscapes, from trees and snakes, from birds and flowers, were commonplace.

The Victorians loved to produce letters that looked as though they were made from other things, from twigs and logs or the shapes of animals and people, or from snow and icicles, flame and fire. They created banners and flags of

Figure 1.3: *Type as decoration. At the top are letters created from broken bits of wood, after the fashion of the French typographer of the 1880s, E. A. Ducompex. Below are five examples where the medium helps reinforce the message. Outline lettering gives users the opportunity to draw within the shape of the letter. Solid lettering can also be treated graphically by superimposing it on a grid of black or white lines. Additional variations can be achieved by reversing images against a black background.*

words, hung letters on washing lines or put them in chains. Art Nouveau artists used windblown letters to suggest storms, sometimes varying shapes from one page to another.

Art Deco lettering is a fantastic mix of geometric machine–age symbols. As they showed, fanciful lettering can communicate as effectively as severe classical forms. In Paris in the 1880s E. A. Ducompex created alphabets made from broken pieces of wood nailed together and from piping, bamboo and metal balls.

Aubrey Beardsley drew curvilinear letters for his edition of Malory's *Morte D'Arthur*. In our own time Erte has invented fantastic alphabets of intertwined people and animals. There is no reason why these should not serve as inspiration for microcomputer treatments.

The modern attitude is that printing should be invisible, no more than a sheet of glass between the reader and the words. For company reports and serious newsletters, where the attention is on the communication of facts, that approach is understandable and has the weight of this century's typography behind it.

Many people are unaware that print need not be straightfoward, for they have not been exposed to anything else. But in some forms of communication, the shape of letters can help carry the message. A typographer will no doubt say that such forms have nothing to do with lettering, but are illustration. To which the only answer is that the pleasure of desktop publishing is that it integrates words and pictures.

Typefaces provided with desktop publishing software or laser printers imitate conventional metal type, just as those, in their turn, copied calligraphy. I don't know why it is that computing is notable for the poverty of its typography.

The letters used in most screen displays are bad and often hard to read, the one type–face created by computerisation – the hi–tech style found on bank cheques – is probably the ugliest ever invented and many dot–matrix printers, left to their own devices, produce horrendous results.

1.9 Designing fonts
There is much pleasure to be got from designing your own fonts, particularly for reproduction with dot–matrix printers – especially when it is an unusual style where elegance is less important than effect. A publication produced with DTP software cannot yet compete in quality with one printed in a conventional manner. But you can do things that are difficult to achieve in

conventional printing, particularly in creating decorative type–styles. It is hard to achieve certain effects in metal for type can be fragile and breaks easily. As we are drawing everything on the screen it is easy to make letters that are individual and different, that can add an element of wit or whimsy to the message.

Early printers produced very decorative work, using woodcuts. These were often crudely drawn, just as the type itself was sometimes rough and uneven. But the finished product still impresses with its vigour, and it is that quality, of vitality and invention, which can be achieved with desktop publishing.

Such styles are not difficult to recreate with a computer. They can add individuality to many kinds of publication. A flysheet from a plumber that puts the words "BURST PIPES?" into water–logged lettering, or from a central heating engineer that has a snow–capped "ARE YOU FREEZING TONIGHT?" will add force to their message.

There are two ways of creating individual typefaces. The first is to design one from the beginning, which is not as difficult as it may sound. The other is to adapt the styles provided with the software. Again, it is easy to transform these so that the word suits the action it describes.

The only problem is one of copyright. Many typefaces are copyright, though it is difficult to understand how it applies to fonts that have existed for hundreds of years, and the owners may object to them being tampered with. You can either adapt fonts that are in the public domain, or design your own based upon the classic style of the past, which can be found reproduced in many books.

You can, for instance, take a sans serif display face and alter its appearance by drawing lines through it, which adds an impression of speed. Such go-faster lines can be drawn at regular intervals through the entire word or through each individual letter.

Such adaptations are quickest done at pixel level, by using the magnification facility to be found in much graphics software. Altering a display heading in this way takes only a matter of a minute or two and can, in the right circumstances, look extremely effective.

In the same way, it's a simple matter to add flames or snow or ice to letters. The quickest way here is to draw on one upright and then to use the software to copy it onto the rest of the letters. Once this has been done, you can use the magnification facility again to clean up any stray pixels and to make whatever alterations you think necessary. It does not take long to create an

RoughiSH sTyLe

Figure 1.4: *Type need not be elegant to be effective. Eye–catching lettering for special display purposes can be created by using conventional type in unusual ways, or by drawing the letters. Above, type used in two unconventional ways: by mixing different fonts and sizes, and by imitating the manner of a kidnap note, a punk style which was once mocked but is now becoming a cliche among graphic designers. Below it is lettering crudely hand drawn, using a mouse, and some graffiti–styled scrawl produced using an airbrush tool from a graphics program, which creates a spray–like effect. In the right context, such styles are a useful means of grabbing attention.*

entire flaming or freezing alphabet in this way, which can be saved to disk so that it is ready for use on other future occasions.

The most versatile of typefaces are the outline ones. These can be filled with patterns or superimposed on backgrounds to create interesting effects. If you enlarge the letters, it is also possible to draw inside them. Providing that you keep such pictures simple, by using silhouettes, you can create some intriguing faces that are effective when used as part of a title.

Creating your own fonts can either be done using a design program, if your software has one, or drawn on the screen in much the same way as any other graphic. Drawing has several advantages. It allows for the creation of elaborate faces that are too big to fit into the grid used in a font designer program and makes it easier to produce a face of exactly the size you require.

With the more expensive DTP software, though, the computer will be able to take an outline of a font in one size and reproduce it in any size you want. Whichever method used, it is probably best to rough out the face on graph paper first, in which each square on the paper represents a pixel on screen. For a computerised face, it is best to avoid delicate curves and angled lines.

The problem letters for dot–matrix reproduction are A, M, N, R, U, V, W, X and Y. You need to try to find an elegant solution to them. You also need access to an encyclopedia of type–faces in order to discover one that you like and which lends itself to computerisation.

No one designs a type face without building on work that has gone before and it would be foolish to try to do so. Even the designers of the most familiar Roman typfaces, such as Garamond, Bodoni and Caslon, whose work adorns many newspapers still, refined the typefaces of their predecessors. Art Nouveau and Art Deco designers in particular stayed away from straight lines and diagonals, often creating unusual Xs and Rs. Their examples can provide solutions that adapt surprisingly well to the style of the dot–matrix printer.

Excellent source–books for typefaces are the paperback series on Lettering, Graphic Arts and Printing published by Dover Books (distributed in Britain by Constable), which cover everything from historic calligraphic alphabets to modern display fonts. Readers are allowed to reproduce them freely.

1.10 The repetitious alphabet
It is as well to follow the example of some typographers, both ancient and modern, and create fonts from as few forms as possible. Drawing and designing fonts on a micro is a quick process, thanks to graphics software,

which enables you to flip or rotate the letters. Many of the letters in an alphabet can be formed from the same basic shape. If you examine a page of Gutenberg's Bible, the first printed book, you'll discover that an "n" is formed by printing the letter "i" twice close together and that the "m" is made up of three "i"s.

So, in designing your own font, you can make use of the similarities of letters. A capital "A" can be an inverted "V" with a vertical line added. A "C" is a "D" reversed and minus its upright, and is also half of an "O" and most of a "G".

An "E", "F", and "L" differ only in the number of horizontal strokes they have. The upright of an "I" appears in a "T" and also forms the two uprights of an "H". A "J" is usually an "I" with a tail on the end. A "Q" is an "O" with a tail. "P" and "R" are closely linked, as are "X" and "Y", "V" and "W". A "Z" can be formed as a mirror–image of an "S".

Once these relationships are noted, it does not take long to adapt one letter to form another. The similarities are not always so obvious with the lower–case alphabet, although they are there.

A lower–case "a" can be turned round to become an "e", a "b" can be easily changed into a "d", a "c" is an "e" without the addition of a horizontal, a "g", "p" and "q" are all variations of each other, "h", "i", "j" use the same upright, "u" with a tail added becomes a "y" and "v" is doubled to form a "w", while "s" and "z" still mirror each other.

If you don't use a font designer, then you should work on a reasonably large scale, as such type–faces will be used for display, to form headlines. First draw a box of around 33 pixels high by 21 wide – odd numbers make it easier to fix the centre of the letter. Mark the centre lines on each side of the box on the outside to provide a guide for the lining up the central point of the letter.

Then copy the box until you have a line of empty boxes in which to draw your letters. Begin with a letter such as a "C", which can be easily adapted to form other letters. Graph paper is useful to work out not merely the shape of the letter, but its thickness.

You will need to make a letter four or five pixels thick in order to achieve a pleasing shape. You only need to work out the shape of one letter – whichever you decide to start with – on the graph paper. Not all letters will be of the same proportions, of course. An "M" and a "W" will be wider than the others. One sample type–face shown here was based on an 1890s Art

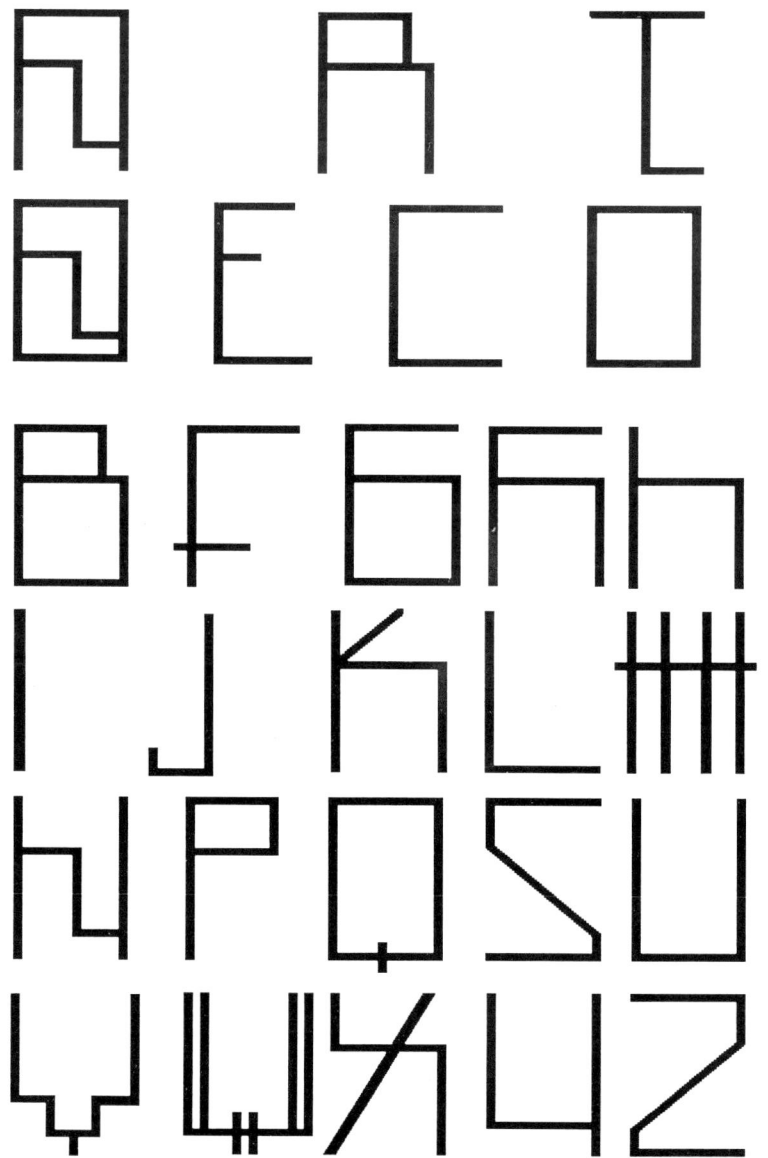

Figure 1.5 *An Art Deco typeface, designed to reproduce well on a dot−matrix printer, with little jaggedness showing in the letters. Such typefaces are not, of course, intended for everyday use, but for specialised display purposes.*

Nouveau design from Germany. It was drawn rather than produced with a font designer since its proportions would not fit satisfactorily within the designer's grid. It was designed on a 33 x 21 grid.

The advantage of such faces over Roman ones when using a dot–matrix printer lies in their lack of jagged lines, and the fact that their size can be increased without producing some of the distortions characteristic of many fonts, which become extremely ragged in outline when made two or four times their usual size. When enlarged, some stepping does occur along the diagonals, but this can be quickly rectified by filling in empty pixels to produce a smooth line.

This particular face was chosen because its shapes lend themselves to computerisation, although the K and the X are more angular than in the original. There are, though, many Art Nouveau faces using a basically rectangular design that are well worth reviving for desktop publishing.

Such faces, of course, look old–fashioned and are not be suitable for all purposes. They would look bizarre in a newsletter styled after a tabloid newspaper, for example. But in the right context, in a publication concerned with the arts for instance, home–made fonts can look good and have the merit of individuality.

It is possible to create very elaborate lettering, from initial letters superimposed on a drawn background to Art Deco ones that combine patterns with the letters. Using a drawn alphabet is not as fast as typing one in from the keyboard, but it does not take long to pick out the letters you require one by one to form a headline (which is how printers did it before the invention of presses using hot metal composition, and is much the same as the technique used with transfer lettering today).

Given the versatility of art programs, there is very little that you cannot do to create unusual type effects, which can be rotated, twisted and slanted to create unusual effects. Elaborate geometric patterns which can used to form unusual backgrounds to letters can be created from simple BASIC programs, the screens saved to disk, and then imported into graphic programs for treatment. When used with a laser printer, such typefaces are treated as bit-mapped graphics and do not reproduce as well as the printer's built–in typefaces. But the standard of reproduction is an acceptable one for many purposes.

1.11 Typographic measurement
Typography has developed its own standards of measurement: points and picas (pronounced pie'kers), which don't quite square with anything else.

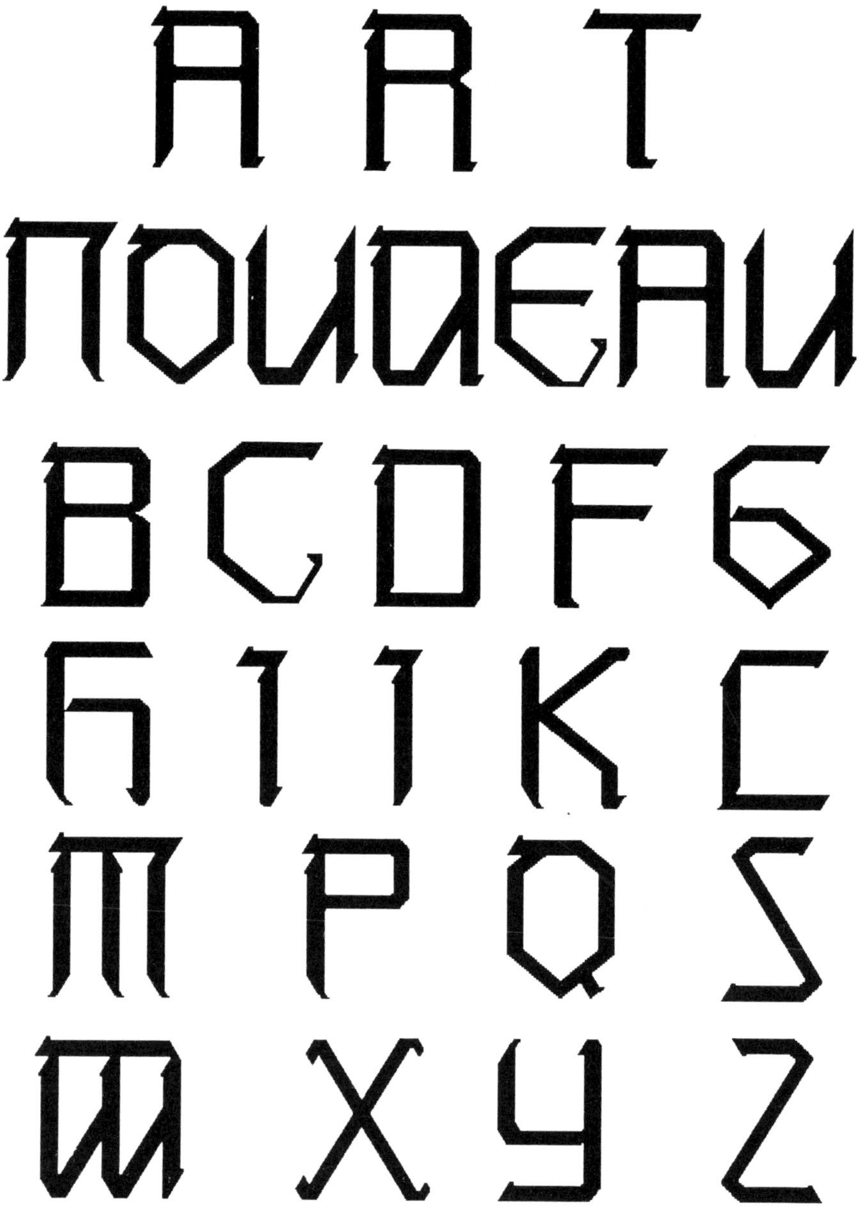

Figure 1.6: *An Art Nouveau font, based upon a German design of the 1890s, a period when type design was undertaken by artists, who brought about radical changes that continue to influence those in search of unusual forms.*

Roughly speaking, there are 72 points to the inch. And there are, more or less, 6 picas to the inch – or, if you prefer, one pica is equal to 12 points. In desktop publishing, these measurement are precise.

Printers refer to 12 point type as pica, just as they talk, or used to, of Double English, which is 24 point type, Great Primer (pronounced prim'er), which is 18 point, English, which is 14 point, Long Primer, which is 10 point, Bourgeois (pronounced bur–joice), which is 9 point, Brevier (pronounced bre–veer), which is 8 point, Minion, which is 7 point, Nonpariel (pronounced non–parel), which is 6 point, Agate, which is five–and–a–half point, Ruby, which is five–and–a–quarter point, and Pearl which is five point.

None of these terms, apart from pica, matter unless you talk to printers who may lapse into a jargon as impenetrable to outsiders as computer–talk. All that it is necessary to know is that the height of a letter is measured in points. The width at which a line of type is set is measured in picas.

There are also measurements which are not absolute, but relative. The most important of these are ens, ems and thins. An en is a space equal to that filled by the letter "n" of a particular font. An em equals to the space filled by the letter "m", which is a square, as wide as it is high. So an en is half an em. A thin is the space occupied by a full stop.

Their actual size will depend upon the size of the letters. In 12 point type an em will be 12 points and an en six points; in six point type, an em will be six points and an en three points. These two measurements are used most often as the basis for indenting lines. A thin is used for spacing letters.

These units of measurements have a relevance to desktop publishing, simply because, for the moment, it apes conventional printing. Fonts available for laser printers are measured in points in the traditional way. Many desktop publishing system provide an option of choosing measurement by inches, centimetres, points or picas.

In conventional printing it is necessary to know how many lines of type will fit on a page, so that an accurate estimate can be made of the amount of space a particular document will occupy. Tables are provided of the number of characters of a particular font that will fit into a pica.

Such calculations are no longer necessary with desktop publishing, since it only takes a few seconds to put the words in a page and see how much space they occupy. Since the text can be put into a page, or pages, and removed speedily, it is a quicker method than carrying out complicated calculations, and is yet another benefit of desktop publishing. It is a good idea, though, to make a note of the number of words it takes to fill a page in the typestyles you use regularly, so that you have some guide to the space required by particular articles when preparing rough layouts of a publication.

1.12 Typographic rules
However inventive you become in your use of type, there are still some guidelines that should be borne in mind:

- Create a coherent style for any particular publication
- Never use more than 3 fonts on a page.
- Restrict unusual styles to headings.

More than anything else, it is the typography that gives a publication its particular feel. Particularly if you're planning a publication that will appear regularly, then you need to spend time working out the fonts you will use and creating rules for their appearance on the page.

There should be some logic or reason behind your selection of a particular type. For instance, you could decide that all main headlines should be 36 points, that subsidiary headings should be 24 points, sub- or cross-heads should be 18 points, that the body text should be 10 points except for the first or second paragraphs, which should be 12 points. Too many fonts on a page are confusing.

Sub- or cross-headings are probably best set in the same typeface as the main text, but in a larger size. Unusual typefaces need to used sparingly, otherwise they cease to be unusual and lose their point. A large slab of text set in an unusual typeface will probably be unreadable or at least discouraging to all but the most determined readers. For that reason, bizarre type is best confined to a heading and should be used appropriately, to accompany out-of-the-ordinary copy.

1.13 Recommended typefaces
The type you decide to use will depend upon not only on what faces attract you, which will probably be ones that have launched a thousand publications, but what is available. The choice may be a restricted one, depending upon the system you use.

For books or pamphlets, excellent faces for the main text are Baskerville, Garamond and Times Roman, which was designed by the great typographer Stanley Morison for The Times Newspaper in 1932. Times Roman, by its nature, is also excellent for the main text in newspapers or magazine-style publications. Times Roman was not the most popular type for newspapers because it required good quality paper and needed careful handling, although neither limitation applies to its use in desktop publishing. Times Bold, the development of Times Roman for headlines, is a good choice for headings, along with Century and Bodoni.

Helvetica is among the most elegant of sans serif faces. Among slab−serifs, Clarendon is effective for headings in flyers or posters. Sans−serif faces, used in their outline or shadowed forms, are eye−catching on posters.

Chapter 2: Style

You need not write well in order to be able to communicate effectively. It helps, of course, but it is not essential, for communication depends more on content than manner. What is important is sticking to a few simple guidelines. Indeed, simplicity is of the essence when putting over your message, whatever it might be.

The main points to keep in mind are:

- Be brief
- Be simple
- Keep to the point

If you want to do more than that, then it is as well to remember that writing is a skill learned by doing. The more you write, the better writer you are likely to become. Brevity helps. If you plan to use a dot-matrix printer to provide your master copy, then brevity is essential since the quality of print is such that it soon becomes wearisome to read.

Unless you're writing a book, try to keep any one piece of writing – whether it is a handbill advertising your services or an annual report – within two A4 pages. Readers are more likely to tackle an article if they can see its end before they begin. Otherwise they will put off reading it until they have more time, and that usually means never. It is not enough to keep the article short. Keep your sentences short. That way, you're less likely to become entangled in subordinate clauses and lose your readers along the way, or wander off the point and confuse them as to what it is you want to say.

This succinctness should be allied to a simplicity of style. Never use two words when one will do (or, to rephrase that in fewer words: use one word instead of two). Avoid cliches like the plague. Use short words rather than long ones, so that you may abstain from an extraneous and copious profusion of prolixity. Avoid jargon and the catchphrases of the moment. One currently much-favoured phrase is "is looking" as in "IBM is looking to increase its share of the desktop publishing market". Either "aims" or "plans" would be preferable.

2.1 The rule is: avoid rules

On the other hand, it is as well to remember that language is a living thing and that those who lay down rules as to its use can soon seem ridiculous. Sixty years ago, one newspaper editor forbade his staff to call a theatrical performance a "show", banned the expressions "week-end" and "New Yorker" and insisted on the use of "diplomatist" rather than "diplomat" and of "wedding trip" rather than "honeymoon".

If you are succinct and straightforward in your writing, then it becomes easier to make your points and your mark. You need to know what you want to say before you say it. If you then say it loud and clear, no one will be in any doubt as to what you mean.

Simplicity applies not only to the structure of the sentence and the use of short words. It also means not using too many adjectives or adverbs. Adverbs are unnecessary. Use adjectives as if they were in short supply. One may add a bright sparkle to your story. Too many will distract even the most diligent, careful and cautious reader.

Paragraphs as well as sentences should be kept short if the article is to be set in newspaper-style columns. Otherwise the text takes on too heavy an appearance on the page. If the text is set across the width of the page, then longer paragraphs will look better. This is a matter of design as much as style and is dealt with more fully in the chapters on layout.

2.2 Other guides

There are a other simple guide-lines that will improve your writing. Sentences should be active rather than passive and should have a person as their subject. If I'd been following those precepts I would have written: You must write sentences which are active rather than passive; you must also have a person as the subject.

Thus, rather than writing "Britain manufactures few computers", you'd write "British manufacturers produce few computers". The difference is small in this instance, but it is an approach that can make your meaning clearer; and it also personalises the statement, which is itself an aid to understanding. The concept of "British manufacturers" is far more concrete than the abstraction "Britain".

As with every rule, you can take these too far. I once worked for an encyclopedia publisher who not only insisted that *every* sentence had to have a person as its subject but also banned the use of the passive, which made it very hard to explain coherently such things as the theory of relativity. This publisher believed that writing should be "warm". By this he meant a tone of voice with which a reader could identify. Warmth in this context tended to verge on the sentimental. It was a way of introducing human interest into factual writing. On one occasion the publisher called an editorial conference because he decided that the word "tigress" in a caption "A tigress with her cubs" was definitely not warm, was, indeed, positively frigid. After much brain–storming, we changed the sentence to read: "A mother tiger with her cubs". You cannot get warmer than mothers.

Warmth is not to be despised. It is an approach that undoubtedly works, having made *Reader's Digest* the world's most popular magazine. Flick through any copy and the headlines radiate human interest: "What's Your Happiness Score?"; "...And God Created Mothers"; "Why I'm Glad To Be 40"; and "How to Stand Up for Yourself " to quote but a few that come to hand. The ultimate *Reader's Digest* headline, the one its editors are longing to use, is said to be "New Hope For The Dead".

All the above headlines stick to the guide–lines of simplicity, brevity and warmth. They also make one point and no more. Whatever you write, you are likely to improve it by doing likewise. Always look at what you have written and ask yourself whether it has a human subject, an active tense and a warm tone. If it has not, then see whether making such changes is an improvement. More often than not, it will be.

2.3 Sub–editing

If you are involved in producing any sort of regular publication, from an annual report to a community newsletter, company or class magazine, then it is likely that you will be concerned with fitting other people's copy into the publication. The same rules apply, with the likely addition that any copy is likely to be improved by cutting. Pruning and condensing will not only save space but improve communication. If you have to pause over any sentence in order to understand it, then it needs changing.

Whatever the subject matter, one rule applies. The most important point should be made first – and in the opening paragraph. You need not only to attract a reader's attention, but to keep it. You may fail in the second, but not until the reader has read the opening lines, so that at least one essential point from the article will have been grasped. A rousing finish, or at least some sentences that sum up the points you wish to make, or the impression you hope to give, will also add to the satisfaction of the readers who have stayed with you to the end of the article.

2.4 Common errors

You will also need to be aware of the rules of grammar. Too much fuss is made of splitting infinitives, of ending sentences with a preposition or beginning one with a conjunction. And to deliberately write in such a style may be more than some readers want to put up with. But so long as your meaning is clear, it is not that important. It is not as if you were expecting to win the Nobel Prize for Literature. What does matter is avoiding those mistakes that can confuse readers. The most common is the use, or rather misuse, of the apostrophe. So widespread is this fault becoming that it is almost more common to find it used incorrectly than correctly. I recently counted 40 wrongly placed apostrophes in one issue of a magazine, not including another dozen in the advertisements.

The apostrophe is used to indicate missing letters in words – don't, mustn't – and also to indicate the possessive case, that something belongs to somebody, as in Nelson's column. An apostrophe followed by an "s" is used to indicate possession with singular and plural nouns. Sometimes the second "s" is dropped with plural nouns or with words ending in an "s", because it sounds better without lots of sibilants.. So it may be "The War of Jenkins' Ear" rather than "Jenkins's", although either is correct.

There is only one exception to "'s" indicating possession and that is "it's", which is an abbreviation of "it is". The apostrophe indicates a missing letter. It is the commonest of errors to confuse "it's" and "its", which is a possessive and means "belonging to it". If in doubt, do not use "it's", but always write "it is". In that way you will never have occasion to use it's with an apostrophe.

You can overuse quotation marks. They should be restricted to indicating that you are quoting someone's direct speech. Do not put them around slang expressions. If the expression conveys what you want to say, then sling it in without drawing particular attention to it. In like manner, exclamation marks should be avoided. They are unnecessary. If you've phrased the sentence correctly, the reader will be able to supply his own surprise.

Another frequent mistake is using "different than" when comparing one person with another. People are different from one another.

Aristocratic titles are a constant source of error. There is, for instance, no such person as Lord Lew Grade, despite what you may read in the newspapers. Lord Grade is Lord Grade.

The use of a christian name after Lord or Lady is restricted to the daughters and younger sons of Dukes and Marquesses (or, if you prefer, Marquises), and to the daughters of Earls, but not to an Earl's younger sons, who are known as the Hon. Whoever. (The eldest sons take their father's second title).

The situation is different with baronets, which is a hereditary title, and knights, which is not. They are called by their full name the first time they are mentioned – Sir John Gielgud, for instance – and after that by their first name – Sir John, never Sir Gielgud. The wife of a knight or baronet, though, is called Lady followed by her married surname.

It is useful when using the name of towns to identify them by county or, in the case of foreign ones, by country as well, in order to avoid confusion, or to identify the area to those whose geographical knowledge may be limited.

There is an Antigua in Gautemala and the West Indies, for instance, a Gloucester in England and America, and at least three different Burnhams in Britain. But do not go as far as the journalist who once wrote, "The Duke of Windsor, Berkshire..."

2.5 A house style
If you are planning to produce a regular publication, then it is essential to draw up a house style, which should apply to every written word in every issue. Consistency is important. It would be confusing, say, to refer to the Libyan leader on one page as Colonel Quaddaffy and on another as Col. Gadaffi, or alternate between Peking and Beijing as the capital of China.

You must make up your mind about the spelling of proper names, the use of abbreviations and so on and then stick to it. It makes sense to draw up a style book, which can be given to contributors and kept as a reminder and a guide. A brief example of the type of material such a style book should cover is included in Appendix C.

2.6 Headlines
Headlines are part of virtually every kind of publication, from "Great Sale Starts Tomorrow!" on an leaflet to "Small Earthquake in Chile – Not Many Dead", to quote the winner of a sub–editors' competition to write the dullest newspaper headline.

It is a perfect example of how not to write one. A headline should be an announcement and a teaser, arousing an interest that the article itself should satisfy. Headlines need to be both informative and intriguing.

Good headlines contain verbs. The best headlines have active verbs. You need to use short words in headlines because there is no room for long ones. Short, crisp headlines in the present tense have more impact than long–winded ones that do not contain a verb.

You can test the truth of this by reading any newspaper or magazine or looking at advertisements. The ones that grab your attention will be sharp and to the point, with active verbs. "Man Bites Dog" is better than "Dog is Bitten By Man" and much, much better than "A Curious Assault" as the heading to such a story. As important as the words is the size of the headline, which will depend both upon its importance in the publication and on the design of the page on which it appears, subjects which are dealt with at greater length in the chapters on layout. A headline over a single column story will need to be two or three lines deep.

As you will get at the most three words within a single column, you need at least two lines in order to say anything sensible. If the headline is over two or three columns, a single line is likely to be sufficient, unless it is of particular importance, when two will suffice. That gives you somewhere between six and ten words for your headline, which should concentrate the mind.

The headline needs to sum up the main point of what you are trying to say beneath it. Whether this is a plea for your services to be used – "Call A1 Plumbers today!" – or a company report – "Chairman announces higher profits" – or a class magazine – "Down with school" – the same rules apply.

In order to be able to write an effective headline, you first need to summarise the point of the piece of prose, whether it's a sales brochure or newsletter feature. If you have written it, that makes it easier, since presumably you know what you were trying to say. If it is someone else's copy, then you need to read it and then write down the main point. You will probably have a sentence of 15 words or so. From that, you can distill your headline by rewriting the sentence in eight or nine words. Leave out the irrelevances, the unnecessary detail and replace the long words by shorter ones.

In headlines, people do not have a disagreement, they row. They do not criticise, they slam. They never announce, but tell or reveal. They do not resign, they quit. There is always a short word that will stand in for several long words. It may not be so accurate; it may lack certain nuances so that it does not convey precisely the meaning you want.

But that does not matter. The copy itself will explain the detail. The headline is a coarse medium. It performs the same function as a newspaper vendor selling his wares, shouting a slogan to attract buyers.

Once you have condensed the essence of the copy, then it should be simple to cast it in the form of a simple sentence, which will be hardly more than a subject followed by a verb in the present tense followed by the object. There may be some occasions when there is not one main point to the copy, but two. In that case, you would need to write a headline that actually consisted of two headlines. The main headline would cover the most important point and there would be a subsidiary headline underneath it. On the page these would be differentiated from each other by being set in different sizes of type, with the subsidiary thought in a smaller size.

After you have written your headline, it is best to read it out loud, to test that you are saying what you mean and that no other meanings are being inadvertently expressed. Ambiguity can creep in, as it did in a famous war-time headline, "German Push Bottles Up Rear", where you need to recognise that push is a noun and not a verb and that bottles is a verb and not a noun.

2.7 Cross-heads

When producing a publication set in columns, you will find that cross- or sub-headings are a necessity. Their purpose is not so much to be read as to break up the body of the type into smaller sections. They are part of the design. For this reason, it is possible to replace them by pure decoration, such as a row of asterisks or stars or a similar typographical flourish.

But as these smaller headings within the text are needed, it makes sense to use them as best you can to add excitement to the page. As much as the main heading, they can act as signposts to the reader.

A cross-heading will consist of no more than two words, which should to be taken from the first or second paragraph that follows it. It is not a good idea to have a long gap between the cross-head and the appearance in the copy of the words used. Readers will become confused, wondering if they've missed the reference.

Instead of summarising the story as a headline does, a cross-head should used words taken directly from the copy. As you will use one or two words only, the cross head will contain a noun, possibly with an adjective, rather than a verb.

Try to choose as evocative a word as possible. "Shock", "Horror" or "Tragedy" are the sort of words that will catch a reader's eye. It is more likely to be something dull, since your choice is limited by your subject-matter. But do try to pick out the most interesting word, even if it is not particularly significant within the context of the article. The point, as with all writing, is to engage a reader's attention. And then to keep it.

Part Two
Pictures

Chapter 3: Graphics

There are several different methods of creating illustrations with a computer. You can use a:

- Business graphics program
- Computer Aided Design (CAD) program
- Art program
- Graphics tablet
- Scanner
- Digitiser

Most of these have limitations that are due to technical difficulties of reproduction. Simply, it is that the quality is poor in comparison with traditional methods of illustration such as photographs or drawings or paintings done by artists.

Dot-matrix printers, traditionally used for computer graphics, have a low resolution. Text produced by laser printers might pass for traditional type-setting, but its graphics output usually gives away its computer-generated origins. A professional artist working on a microcomputer is likely to produce less interesting work than when using a pen, pencil or brush. Conversely, someone with little artistic skill can produce an acceptable quality of work by using a computer.

No illustration that you can produce with a computer can compare with the quality of a good photograph. This does not mean that computer graphics have no place in desktop publishing. Most publications are improved by the addition of illustrations.

Graphics do need to be used with care. Many times, even when using computerised illustrations, you will find it beneficial to produce the graphics separately, leaving a space of the right size in your page make-up and then sticking down the illustration after you have printed the page, or supplying a photographic transparency to the printer to be added to a typeset page. Computer graphics have some advantages over conventional illustrations. The most important is that the final image is not fixed. It can very easily be made bigger or smaller, rotated at an angle, have any text changed in caption, font, or size. Indeed, there is no end to the ways you can alter the image.

Another asset is that people not skilled in art can still produce acceptable images on a computer since the tools available make it so simple. Giotto

Chapter 3

might have been able to draw a perfect circle freehand, but not many others can. A computer art program will allow you to draw geometric shapes such as circles, ellipses, rectangles and triangles automatically.

Some DTP software has a built-in art program to allow you either to create images or to make changes to ready-made illustrations. With other programs, you need to create the image with an art program, such as *MacDraw* on the Macintosh or Digital Research's *GEM Draw* on IBM and compatible PCs. But not all graphics programs are compatible with DTP software.

With most DTP packages there is available a selection of drawings, usually referred to as clip art. These are the equivalent of illustrations, in the form of transfers or cut outs, that are used for producing advertisements or general illustrations in small town newspapers.

Computerised clip art is cut out and pasted into position electronically. Available images, depending on the package you decide to use, range from Walt Disney characters to maps and credit card logos. Clip art can either be used as it comes or changed in various ways within a graphics program.

In order to produce drawings that look as if they were done freehand, resembling pen or pencil sketches, you need to use a drawing program linked to a graphics tablet. Such additional hardware, together with the use of digitisers and scanners, is dealt with in the next chapter.

Graphic programs can be divided into two kinds:

- Bit-mapped
- Object-orientated.

Bit-mapped graphics work on one level. If you alter a line, or fill-in an outline shape, it stays altered or filled-in.

Object-orientated programs treat the graphic shapes as separate objects so that you can lay one drawing down on top of another without changing either. CAD programs, where complex drawings can be built up by overlaying several plans, are object-orientated.

3.1 Business Graphics

Business graphics programs are designed to produce graphs and charts. They can be used on their own or linked with spreadsheets to provide a graphic version of its numerical data. Some spreadsheets do have built-in graphics for this purpose, but they are usually of poorer quality than programs

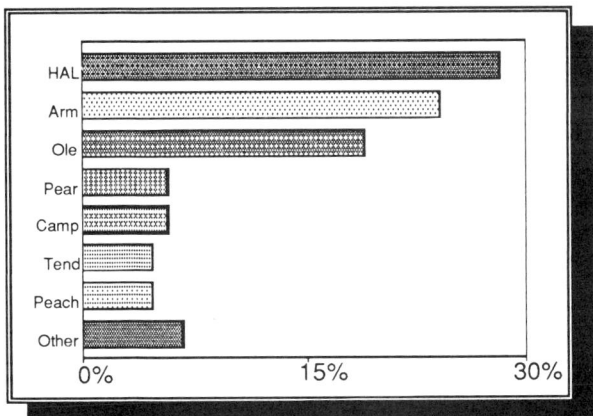

Microcomputer Sales 1990

Figure 3.1: *A simple bar chart, above, can add useful graphical information to newsletters and company reports, as well as improving the look of the page.*

designed to do nothing else but output charts. Within the context of desktop publishing, these are more successful than any other kind of computer graphics. Graphs present the same problem as graphs produced by any other method: they can be difficult for the uninitiated to understand.

But pie and bar charts, which convert numerical data into easily understood graphical shapes, are extremely successful and of great use in any desktop publishing connected with business. Computerised charts of this kind are quick to produce. Once the data, of sales figures or market shares and the like, is entered, the computer instantaneously calculates the size of the bars or the individual portion of the pie.

You then select various tints or shading to represent different data, and the chart is ready in much less time than it would take a person to calculate and draw it. The finished chart can be scaled to whatever size you require. The result is effective, since the chart supplies easily–assimilated information. Most computer graphics are more decorative than informative.

You can improve the presentation of business graphics by combining them with suitable illustrations. If you were displaying a chart of the rise in drinking among the young, for instance, you could add a drawing of a pub scene or even use bottles instead of bars in the chart. Another approach would be to frame the graph within the outline of a bottle. Such tricks enliven the page.

3.2 CAD software

If you need to produce detailed plans, designs for rooms or elevations of buildings, then Computer Aided Design programs are essential. These are intended for use by architectural or engineering draughtsmen and produce accurately–scaled line drawings.

CAD programs also allow you to draw three dimensional shapes and manipulate them, turning them to any angle you want. This can be useful in the production of technical manuals for showing the same object as it would be seen from different positions.

CAD programs are designed to work in conjunction with a plotter, a arm holding one or more pens which draws under the computer's control. Printed output from plotters is of high quality. If used in conjunction with desktop publishing, you may find it best to produce the print with a plotter and then paste it into position on a finished page.

If the DTP package does not include many graphic facilities, or even if it does, what do you need? Specific graphics software is discussed more fully in the next chapter. A fairly simple program will suffice.

You are more likely to be printing in black and white so that programs that offer various ways of mixing or smearing colours, or creating colour washes are not required.

3.3 Art programs

What you require is a program that can automatically generate simple geometric shapes, since complex drawings can be built up from such shapes. You need a program that will accept text, for it can be very useful to change the appearance of words by shrinking, stretching or rotating them.

You need to be able to manipulate shapes in the same way. Most important is the ability to copy, and to move around the screen, part of the picture, a facility which can save a great deal of drawing. You need also to be able to add tints, textures and patterns. A simulated airbrush, which allows you to spray a pattern of dots on the screen can be useful for adding shading.

Art programs usually let you draw freehand, but since this is done by moving either a mouse or a joystick, the control you have is minimal and the results will be poor – unless you want a lot of scribbling on the screen. Illustrations produced with the aid of a graphics program will tend to be hard-edged and will have a something of a mechanical feel about them. If reproduced with a dot-matrix printer they will also have the usual problem of jagged lines and stepping in circles and ellipses.

Perhaps the really essential requirement for an art program is its ability to magnify part of the image on which you are working. You need to be able to zoom in so that you can change the picture at pixel level. A pixel, a word that is an abbreviation of picture element, is a single dot of the many from which your picture is composed.

Pixels are used as the unit of measurement for the resolution of the screen or the printed picture. The two are not necessarily the same. Some CAD programs produce a resolution of 1024 x 1024 dots when the result is printed, although the resolution on the screen may be no more than 640 x 400 pixels.

Being able to draw at pixel level is of great benefit to an unskilled artist. You can add fine detail easily. You can tidy up elements of the picture, adding or removing shading. You can also draw virtually anything, although it can take time. The best graphics programs display the image as it is normally seen and the magnified section on which you are working simultaneously so that you can see the effects of the changes you are making.

Although computerised drawings, apart from business graphics or CAD views of a plan or a product, provide little immediate information, they are a useful means of adding some decorative content to the page.

3.4 Logos and symbols
The graphics that work best are those providing a stark contrast between black and white. Aubrey Beardsley, whose Edwardian drawings used bold lines and blocks of black, would have made a splendid computer artist. A successful computer-graphics technique is closer to engraving or woodcuts than the usual methods of drawing.

Logos or symbols can be used successfully in newsletters or magazine-style publications to indicate regular columns or the coverage of particular subjects. Shapes in black silhouette, when surrounded by white space can look dramatic on the page. You can use such images effectively on a small scale, which also makes them quick and easy to draw.

Arrows or pointing fingers can be used to draw a reader's attention to a particular part of a publication. You can, of course, over-use such devices. Too many of them on a page will only confuse the eye. Such symbols are more commonly used than they used to be. *The Guardian* newspaper, for

Figure 3.2: *Symbols and logos can enliven pages. The above examples come from the clip art supplied with Gold Disk's* PageSetter *desktop publishing software.*

instance, uses them to add variety to its sports and feature pages: stylised balls next to coverage of rugby, soccer and cricket, a pair of gloves for its boxing coverage, a blackboard on its Education pages, and so on. They have also become part of computer consciousness as icons used by the Macintosh's operating system or Digital Research's GEM (Graphics Environment Manager) on the IBM PC and Atari ST.

Used throughout a publication as signposts to readers they add not only an additional design interest to the page, but can help give a publication a sense of unity and coherence. Even those users who cannot draw ought to be able to create such symbols with the drawing tools that an art program provides.

3.5 An exercise in graphics

To take a simple example, involving someone lacking in the skills of draughtmanship. My task was to create a letterhead, using a simple DTP program (*Fleet Street Editor* running on Acorn's 8–bit BBC micro), which was to be printed on a dot–matrix printer. It was to include not only the name and address but a drawing of the house, which was fortunately (or maybe unfortunately) exceedingly elegant, being one of the thirty identical houses that forms the Georgian Royal Crescent in Bath. Before beginning I examined many prints of the Crescent produced by various artists over the two hundred or so years since it was built, and made an interesting discovery.

Few of the prints actually resembled the Crescent as it is or was. The artists had not been hampered by sticking to what they saw. They had simplified. In one case, presumably because of artistic incompetence, the gentle curve of the Crescent had been drawn as a block, as if it were a side of the square. In another, a river had been added close by, although actually it is a long way off.

I had learned my first lesson. If something is hard to draw ignore it, or change it. It is the overall impression that matters, not the detail. I decided that the drawing should be framed on one side by the house that forms the beginning of the Crescent and, on the other by a tree. There are trees near the Crescent, but none in the position where I put one.

In showing only part of the Crescent, I saved myself drawing the whole sweep of 30 houses. As a result, I did not need to draw the houses on a curve, which was beyond my capabilities and which also would print with jagged lines.

The house at one end was built up as a succession of rectangles, which the computer drew automatically. The pillars were rectangles with their capitals drawn as small rectangles on top. Then, drawing at pixel level, these were rounded. Shading was added, using the program's pattern fill to give the impression of roundness.

One house was drawn in the same manner, from a succession of rectangles, and then copied to provide a row of houses. Then the shading was added to the roof, using the program's facility to fill a shape with a pattern.

Then came the tree. I made several attempts to draw a tree, all of which were extremely unsuccessful. Going back to look at some old engravings for inspiration, I noticed that the artists' trees were impressionistic, built up from textures. But how could I create a suitable texture?

I went through the clip art included with the program and found a drawing of a frog and a lizard. I copied a chunk of the lizard's body, copied it again and again and I had a nicely textured tree trunk. I used the same technique of copying part of the frog's body to form the foliage. Using the magnification function, I removed some of the pixels to give the edges a more leafy look. After that, I added the name and address, using a font supplied with the

Figure 3.3: *An exercise in graphics. It begins as a few rectangular shapes and ends as a letterhead.*

program that resembled handwriting. As it looked as if it were rather floating in the space, I drew a simple bird–like shape beneath to contain it.

The result, shown on the preceding page, is far from even competent art. But it works well enough. It has a sort of naive charm and, thanks to the graphics facilities included within *Fleet Street Editor*, was not difficult to do and took one–and–a–half hours to complete.

3.6 Borders and capitals
Most DTP software allows you to frame text or graphics in boxes. These tend to be simple, made up of one or two thick or thin black lines. There are occasions when more elaborate borders are required.

You can not only copy images in any good graphics program, but also mirror them on their different axes, which means that you need only draw one corner to create four corners and just a section of the border, which can be copied to join them. Art Deco provides a good source of geometric designs which are simple to produce with the graphics tools available.

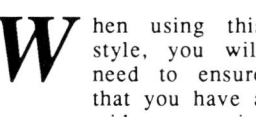

Cock–up is the term used for the setting where the capital rises above the rest of the text.

When using this style, you will need to ensure that you have a wide margin.

DROP initial letters may look best when the rest of the word is also set in capital letters.

Figure 3.4: *Three ways of setting initial capital letters. The letter set above the others, or cocked–up, is usually found in books. The side–setting requires space to look effective.*

Fancy drop capitals, which can also form an effective means of decoration on a page, can be created with no difficulty, since you can superimpose any letter on a pattern or drawn background and put a frame around it. On most computers you can capture any image from the screen, transfer it to a graphics program and manipulate it to form a pattern or background for unusual effects.

A graphics program is an essential aid to desktop publishing and is the cheapest way of creating individual designs. If you are producing any publications within a business, then a graphics program for drawing graphs and charts is also a necessity. Other methods of illustration require the addition of expensive hardware.

Chapter 4: Graphic Aids

The problem with desktop publishing is that the pictures are not worth a thousand words. They are short on information. Nevertheless, the graphic possibilities of desktop publishing can be extended by adding such peripherals as graphics tablets, scanners and digitisers.

4.1 Graphics tablets

A graphics tablet is the best way to achieve freehand drawing with a computer. An alternative is to use a light pen, with which you draw directly on the screen. Software supplied with light pens resembles your average art program, allowing you to manipulate the image you create and also to draw geometric shapes and straight horizontal and vertical lines automatically. The difficulty comes with using a light–pen, since a vertical screen is not the best–placed surface for freehand drawing.

Using a graphics tablet, on the other hand, is more like drawing on a flat sheet of paper, and can be used to create line drawings that resemble pen or pencil sketches. Instead of using a tracker ball, joystick or keyboard with which to draw, you use a pencil or a stylus, which resembles a blunt pencil, or a puck, which is more like a mouse fitted with a cross–hair sight.

By moving the stylus or puck over the surface of the tablet, you produce a drawing on the screen. It is a method that enables you to exercise fine control over the lines you draw. You can also trace around existing drawings, such as maps, in order to reproduce them on the screen.

4.2 Digitisers

Digitisers are a way of capturing photographs and then manipulating them, playing around with them in the same manner as any other computerised image. They use a video camera or capture images from a television, video recorder or a laserdisc player.

This raises some interesting questions of copyright, since a still image taken from a film or a programme is not yours, unless you have sought, and been given permission, by the copyright holders. It belongs to the film or television company. Yet after changes have been made, the image is no longer the one that was copyrighted. What its precise standing in law is has not yet been tested.

I suppose you can rest easy, knowing that no one is likely to object to the use of a single image. However, much will depend upon what you do with it.

Some clip art is protected by copyright. For instance, the Walt Disney characters licensed to Mirrorsoft can only be used in non-commercial situations, and even then have to carry the Disney trademark.

A digitiser typically consists of hardware that plugs into the computer, and software that enables you to obtain the best possible picture. Some digitisers work with black and white cameras only, using a system of red, green and blue filters to add colour to the image. Such equipment can be used to capture still images only, since it requires to be focused for twenty seconds on the object to be captured.

Many digitisers take several seconds to digitise an image so that they cannot take images from a television programme, although they can from a video recorder with a freeze-frame facility. Others can capture images instantaneously, or at least at an appromixation of it, taking no more than a sixtieth of a second.

Once the digitiser has taken the image, it makes of it a picture composed of pixels, or picture elements, which is how a computer constructs graphics. The electronic information of the original image is turned into digital data.

In an ideal world, the number of pixels in the original picture would equal the number in the digitised copy. But the resolution of the original is likely to be better than the digitised image, except with the most expensive equipment. It requires considerable memory to be able to hold enough information to create a convincing monochrome image composed of different levels of grey.

At their very best, digitisers can display images in a resolution that approaches that of a photograph. The problem remains in printing it, when the resolution is limited by the printer. For that reason, the final result tends to be mediocre in quality. By manipulating the image, you can obtain some interesting results and some striking illustrations. But they will not convey as much information as the original images.

4.3 Scanners
Scanners work rather like dot-matrix printers in reverse. You feed in a piece of paper containing an image, which is scanned by a beam of light. A photosensor detects the amount of light being reflected, assigns to it a value on a scale of shades of grey and reproduces it on the screen.

Some scanners are self-contained units. Others actually replace the ribbon cartridge in a printer. Scanning graphics can be a slower process than printing a picture and can take as long as twenty minutes with low-cost devices. The more expensive scanners will complete the process in around 60 seconds. The results vary from the moderate to the excellent. The best scanners, though, will cost even more than a laser printer.

Scanning works best with originals that display high contrast. Some scanners will automatically enlarge or reduce the original image. By means of software you can make alterations in the contrast and brightness of the image after the scanning has finished.

If you intend printing with a laser printer, then, in order to achieve the best results, you need to ensure that the scanner's resolution matches the printer's resolution of 300 dots per inch. Otherwise, the image will look no better than if it were reproduced on a dot−matrix printer.

Scanners can be used to enter text, which can then be transferred to a word processor or loaded in a DTP system for editing. But their application is likely to be limited to a few typewriter typefaces and they will not work with printed pages from books or magazines. Their accuracy varies but rarely reaches perfection so that you will need to check scanned copy carefully, for words will be misspelt or extraneous characters introduced.

Scanners use Optical Character Recognition (OCR) as the means of transferring words from the page to the computer. This is a relatively unsophisticated method in which the computer holds in memory the shapes formed by different characters and then matches what it reads on the page with the pattern in memory.

Such machines are easily confused by poorly formed letters and can read only specific fonts. The latest scanners use a different method in which characters are analysed according to their individual shapes and the relationships between their various parts so that, in theory at least, a letter can still be recognised when printed in different fonts and in different sizes.

In practice, scanners are still easily confused. Many cannot deal with proportionately space text, for instance, or italic faces. They can cope only with the most common typewriter styles, such as Courier, Pica and Elite, and with the output from typewriters or daisywheel printers rather than from dot−matrix machines.

Copy needs to be cleanly presented and is fed into the scanner one sheet at a time. Scribbled notes or corrections in pen or pencil are a disaster. Despite these limitations, scanners can be useful for entering text that exists only in typewritten form, or for getting copy from contributors into the computer. Ideally, though, you should try to ensure that all contributions to any publication created by DTP software are supplied on floppy disk using a word processor compatible with your desktop publishing system. Otherwise, a great deal of time will be wasted.

4.4 Graphics software

There are a great many graphics programs on the market and more appearing every day. Many are useful adjuncts to desktop publishing. What follows is a brief look at some of the best from a desktop publishing point of view. Some excellent art programs are omitted because their advantages, such as brilliant use of colour, are of no practical use for our purposes, and will not be until colour desktop publishing becomes a practical possibility. More useful for desktop publishing are programs that allow you to manipulate and distort images and text.

4.4.1 Macintosh software

MacPaint quickly established itself as the leading art program in the early days of the Macintosh, when it was bundled with the computer. It is weakest in creating special effects, though its shortcomings can be overcome by *Click Effects*, an extra program that enables images to be stretched, slanted and rotated.

A newer rival is *FullPaint*, which has the advantage of allowing four drawings to be on−screen at the same time so that you can move images from one to the other. It also allows operations of stretching, distorting, skewing and perspective to be carried out. For quality DTP purposes, *Cricket Draw* is possibly the better buy since it is *PostScript* compatible and designed to work with Apple's LaserWriter. It can bend text to follow a curved line and create complex shading effects.

There are several specialised and expensive CAD programs, such as *MacArchitrion*, for architectural plans, and *E−Z Draft*. A cheaper alternative is *MacDraft*, which allows accurate drawing and provides good quality reproduction when used with a laser printer. There is available a vast library of clip art for the Macintosh, ranging from maps and unusual display fonts to business forms, invoices, statements, credit notes and the like. (For further details, see the Reference Guide.)

Because of the Mac's graphics−orientated approach to computing, it is usually possible to transfer images between programs, so that the amount of ready−made art which can be used in DTP packages is vast.

4.4.2 IBM software

The IBM PC, and the many compatible computers which ape it, are not noted for their graphic capabilities. The DTP packages for it make use of one or other of its two graphics–orientated interfaces, Microsoft's Windows or Digital Research's GEM to provide a display similar to that of the Macintosh.

Windows will form part of the operating system for the newest generation of IBM PCs. GEM creates a compatible environment for most software that runs under it. Of the two leading DTP systems for the IBM, *Ventura Publisher* runs under GEM and *PageMaker* under Windows.

No graphics program for the IBM matches what is possible with the Macintosh or the Commodore Amiga. They are, so far, inferior and harder to use. With *Ventura*, it makes sense to use *GEM Paint* and *GEM Draw*, which has CAD facilities, for drawing and *GEM Graph* for producing business graphics.

Microsoft's *Chart 2.0* produces with reasonable ease graphs and charts of eight different types (area, bar, column, hi–lo, line, mixed, pie and scatter) which can be displayed in various formats.

4.4.3 Amstrad CPC software
DTP packages for the CPC include drawing facilities and graphics manipulation so that extra programs are not essential. Running under CP/M, *DR Draw* is a CAD program and *DR Graph* provides business graphics, although you would need to use cut and paste methods to integrate them with the available DTP software.

4.4.5 Amstrad PCW software
The two DTP packages available at the time of writing for Amstrad's word processing computer, *Fleet Street Editor Plus* and *The Desktop Publisher*, both incorporate graphics editors that will meet most users' requirements. (It is odd that inexpensive DTP software usually includes graphics facilities that are not found in more expensive programs.)

Fleet Street Editor Plus contains a graphics editor that allows the user to add text to drawings, and also to manipulate images by re–sizing and rotating them. *The Desktop Publisher's* graphics are less comprehensive, but adequate. For CAD drawings or business graphics, *DR Draw* and *DR Graph* are useful programs.

4.4.6 Atari ST software
Both DTP packages available for the Atari ST, *Fleet Street Publisher* and *Publishing Partner*, run under GEM and have the same drawing features as well as the ability to re–size images. A greater degree of manipulation of images can be achieved with some good graphics software. *Art Director* has

interesting features that allow you to rescale, stretch, bend, rotate and completely distort images. There is also an unusual bulge command which takes an image and curves it so that it looks at though it is viewed in a distorting mirror. A flat image can also be transformed into one displayed in perspective, which can be used to create some striking effects.

Art Director includes several fonts and allows you to design your own fonts for use within the program. It is compatible with the Pro–Draw Graphics Tablet, the Haba Video Digitiser, and *Fleet Street Publisher. Degas Elite* – the title does not refer to the French impressionist painter but is an acronym for Design and Entertainment Graphics Art System – is an excellent and versatile program, although it lacks the perspective feature of *Art Director*. But it does match it in other ways of manipulating an image.

4.4.7 BBC B/Master/Compact
The two best DTP programs for the BBC micros, *Fleet Street Editor* and *Stop Press*, which were written for the 32K BBC B, contain graphics programs that will meet most requirements. Because BBC software uses a variety of incompatible graphics modes, there is available for both packages a utility to convert images from one graphics mode to another so that they can be used with the programs.

The most advanced graphics package for the BBC micro remains *AB2*, which was produced by a graphic designer for his own use. It has a number of useful advanced features such as stretching or shrinking images or text, quick three–dimensional drawing and shading and the automatic drawing of complex patterns through seven predefined points. Other useful software includes *Hershey Characters*, which allows you to print words on the screen in a range of typefaces and in a variety of ways, such as slanted or rotated. The messages on the screens can then be saved and loaded into DTP packages.

Graphito contains a variety of programs permitting a wide range of graphics manipulation, such as printing text on cubes or repeating images at different sizes and angles. Once again, the screen image can be saved to disc and loaded into available DTP software. The most versatile CAD program is *Diagram*, which allows you to build up a plan on a scrolling screen and to print it in different sizes. *Inter–Chart*, part of a group of integrated programs that include a spreadsheet and a word processor, produces good quality graphs and charts.

4.4.8 Commodore Amiga software
The Commodore Amiga has the best graphics programs available for any personal computer. An extra advantage is that all virtually all of its graphics

software uses an agreed system of storing images, known as IFF (Interchange File Format), which means that a picture created on one program can be loaded into another.

This sensible attitude has resulted in the availability of a great number of ready–made images for use with the DTP software, although the only program so far available, *PageSetter*, does include a good graphics editor which has most facilities; it does not, however, permit the user to rotate images or to slant them.

The best graphics package is *Deluxe Paint II* from Electronic Arts, which is probably the most advanced package yet written for any personal computer. Its use of perspective allows you to grab any part of the screen, rotate the grabbed image on its axes and arrange it in relation to any chosen vanishing point. There is also a variety of graduated shadings that you can use to fill shapes. Images and text can be altered in all conceivable, and some hitherto unthinkable, ways.

Aegis Images is another powerful easy–to–use graphics creator, and *Aegis Impact* and *Aegis Draw* are comprehensive business graphics and CAD programs.

4.4.9 Commodore 64/128

The best graphics program is Rainbird's *Art Studio*, although probably the easiest to use is the *Koala Painter* program controlled by the Koala Pad, a basic graphics tablet. *Art Studio*, which is also compatible with the Koala Pad, includes a font editor and allows you to zoom in to pixel level to add detail to drawings.

CRL's *The Image System* provides the most comprehensive means of manipulating text and images, allowing some fancy distortions. The creation of three dimensional images, which can be manipulated in various ways, can be achieved with Glentop's *3–D Graphics Drawing Board*. For business graphics, *Chartpak* is as good as any.

Part Three
Design

Chapter 5: Layout

There is only one rule when it comes to layout; and that is there are no rules. Or, rather, the rules are there to be broken. Fashions in layout change, though so imperceptibly that few notice. Readers usually think their newspaper or magazine has always looked the way it does now.

It is only when they compare a recent issue with one of five or ten years ago that they realise the changes that have been made. What was considered reprehensible then is regarded with admiration now. What was regarded as virtually God–given, handed down on tablets of stone, by one group of designers now will be thought of as mildly eccentric by another.

5.1 Different styles
For example, British newspaper designers will tell you that the main focus of attention on the front page is the top left–hand corner, and that it is there that the most important story of the day should be placed.

American newspaper designers, on the other hand, insist that it is to the top right–hand corner that the reader's eye is drawn and they place the main story in that position. So it is, when Britons and Americans read each others newspapers, that they misunderstand the emphasis of the news.

In a similar fashion, British newspapers tend to have one or two photographs on their front page. The tabloid papers will also have no more than one or two stories, and the larger broadsheet newspapers will use a symmetrical layout, in which the left–hand side of the page balances the right–hand side and the bottom complements the top. There will be only one or two different typefaces used, so that the result will suggest genteel restraint.

In contrast, French and Italian popular newspapers will cram eight or nine different photographs on their front pages, use a dozen or more typefaces and scatter exclamation marks, or astonishers, among the headlines like confetti! The result is busy and, for those unused to it, confusing. Such pages break all the rules formulated by British designers, who tend to scorn such exuberance as "circus makeup". Yet French and Italian readers delight in such exuberance.

It all proves that one person's neat layout is another's poison. So, it is worth bearing in mind that if it looks right to you, then it is right. The point of design is to put over your message in as dramatic a way as possible. As scribes and the early printers showed, there is no reason why you should not provide pleasure as well, by adding decoration. It is one of the great advantages of computerised layout over more conventional methods of printing and publishing that decoration is easy to add.

In most magazines and newspapers design is unobtrusive. You do not know it is there, it is so invisible. The last time that design forced itself on readers' attention was in the 1960s, in the newspapers and magazines produced by the so-called "underground press", in which uninhibited young designers played with the freedoms of photocomposition, printing text in coloured inks, adding tints to pages, experimenting with weird and wonderful typefaces, to the consternation of the conventional.

Like many of those attracted to the possibilities of desktop publishing, the underground journalists were amateurs, often unaware that there were rules to be broken. Their approach, of trying anything that takes your fancy, is probably the best one. You cannot compete with the professionals on the printed quality of your work. But you can produce work that is original and individual, that is fun to do and a pleasure to read.

The purpose of design is to communicate, and if you can communicate your own joy in producing your publication, then that will take you a long way to meet your readers, whatever the limitations of the medium. You have at your disposal words, in text and headlines, a variety of typestyles, pictures and another decorative devices.

There are, though, limitations imposed by the available equipment, notably the printers. Even if the software is capable of producing larger than usual layouts, you are likely to find that printing technology limits you to A4 or smaller. A4 – 8.27 x 11.69 ins or 210 x 297 mm – and A5 – 5.83 x 8.27 ins or 148 x 210 mm – are the commonest sizes. It is possible to produce publications of a larger size, but this requires the use of scissors and paste (and will be dealt with in a later chapter).

A5 is best used for something that can fit on to one page: a poster for a local drama group's latest production or announcing a lost cat, a leaflet to put through people's letter boxes informing them of a jumble sale or offering your services as a plumber, electrician or builder – something short and pithy. A5 publications are probably best done in a poster-style: with the page treated as a wide single column, with one large headline, with important information in a prominent position and with possibly a decorative border around it.

Although A4 is still a small size, it is far more flexible and can be used for virtually any sort of publication, from a parish magazine to company reports and memoranda and the local equivalent of *samizdat* literature, such as a book of poems, or even a novel, printed and published by its author. The page–size means that magazines rather than newspapers offer the best models. Indeed, the easiest way to learn effective layout is to copy the design of a publication you admire.

5.2 Essential questions
Most publications conform to certain rules. They contain items of news or information of particular interest. They also contain regular features that probably make up the bulk of the publication.

The regulars would include such matters as hints and tips: whether on the best way to tie a granny knot in a scouting publication or an effective method of nutting a granny in a mugger's newsletter; recipes of various kinds (101 ways with baked beans or how to cook the books); advice columns; letters to the editor; news of members and so on.

It helps if such regular features are marked out from one another. Probably the most effective is by the use of suitable logos. You need to devise distinctive headings which can appear in every issue, providing a feeling of continuity. It may be best to reserve a particular typeface for the headings on regular features in order to emphasise a unity of style.

Before you begin to design your newsletter or magazine, you should have information to hand concerning the content of a particular issue. You need to be able to answer the following questions:

1. How many articles are you planning to use? Do you have enough space to use them all once you've assigned the necessary room to the regular features. If you've too much text, what will you do? Cut the articles? Discard some? Keep some for the next issue?

2. How long are they? In conventional publishing, articles are typeset first so that the length of the copy can be measured and then pasted down in position on the page, or the type itself arranged in a forme that holds the text of all the articles that make up the page. But with desktop publishing, the quickest method is to feed the words into blank pages arranged in columns in the format of the publication and see how much space they occupy.

3. What are your main illustrations? How much space do they need? Are the illustrations computer–generated graphics or will you be adding photographs and drawings? If so, how big are the gaps you need to leave?

4. What is your main story? Roughly speaking, it should occupy more space than the other stories. Are there illustrations to accompany it? If not, how will you mark its importance on the page?

5. Which is the strongest illustration? Will you put it on the cover, if you have one, or on your opening page? Obviously, it make sense to have some picture that relates to your main item of news.

The form of your publication will depend upon the content. There might be some matter of such importance that it would occupy an entire issue.

5.3 The front page

The front page sets the style and tone for a publication. It is what the reader sees first so that its purpose must be to encourage him or her to pick it up and start to peruse it. There are two approaches to a front page. The first is to follow the style of most magazines and have a poster–style cover. This consists of a title along the top and an attractive illustration combined with an indication of the goodies to be found inside: the cover lines, with their come–on, read me messages.

The other approach is that commonly adopted by newsletters and newspapers, which is to have the title at the top and, beneath it, reports on the main events. This may also include a box or boxes giving details of the contents to be found on other pages.

Which approach you take depends on the type of publication you are producing. A poster–style opening is the most difficult, partly because it is not easy to create attractive page–sized illustrations within desktop publishing. Writing effective cover lines is also a skill not easily acquired.

Of course, if cost is not the first consideration, attractive full colour covers can be created and printed in the conventional way, with DTP packages used to produce the remainder of the publication. It is easy to add a single colour – say, for the title – at the printing stage with another publication produced with desktop publishing software. But a front page that depends upon an illustration for its impact may cause more trouble than it is worth.

It is best not to imitate the style of magazines that display their cover lines over the graphic if you are using a dot–matrix printer. Its limitations mean that the lines will be difficult to read, thus defeating their purpose. If you do have an illustration, then it is best to put the cover lines beneath it, or put them in a box against a white or lightly shaded background.

Alternatively, of course, you can provide an effective cover by using typographical means only, listing the contents one by one in a bold typeface, with perhaps a line or two of additional explanation in a smaller type. A title in a fancy typestyle and a border around the outside of the cover would add a decorative touch. The newsletter or newspaper approach is simpler, gets down to the purpose of spreading information without wasting time and saves on space.

Layout will follow the regular pattern for the publication, with the addition of the title at the top. This should be set in type big enough to catch the eye. It may need the date and edition or volume number of the publication beneath it. The title needs to be separated from the rest of the publication by being ruled off with one or two lines across the page.

The important point is to ensure that the relationship between the title and the headlines beneath it should be a harmonious one. You can help to achieve this by using for the title a typeface that appears nowhere else in the publication: anything from Black letter to Art Deco, depending upon your tastes and purposes.

It needs to be distinguished from the surrounding text. You can try different methods to see which looks best: surround it by a decorative border, put a tint behind it, reverse it in white letters out of black, use shadowed or italic lettering.

Remember that Black letter should be set in upper—and—lower case. Titles using a face that resembles handwriting can add both a touch of informality and urgency to a publication and will not clash with the headline style below. Typefaces that resemble stencilled lettering can also be effective as titles.

5.4 Advertisements

You will soon discover that pleasant—looking pages are not too difficult to design; what screws up layout is advertisements, and they are not likely to be your problem. If you do hope to make money, or at least cover costs, by including adverts in your publication, then you need to be aware of the difficulties they can cause. The size and the placement of them on the page are the first of your difficulties.

An advertisement can easily overwhelm the editorial content of a page. It is best to put limits on their size and shape — to, say, no more than half—a—page or a single column on a page. You could even try grouping the advertisements at the back or the front of the publication, so giving a freer run to editorial matter.

Unfortunately, advertisers tend not to like the practice. They prefer their adverts to be next to, or opposite, editorial in the belief that more people are likely to read them and take notice of what they are selling. Advertisements can add to the interest of any publication, so providing an extra service to your readers. But they need keeping in their place. If you're lucky enough to find advertisers, then keep their contribution within strictly defined limits, at no more than a third of the content of the publication, so that readers won't throw it aside after a cursory glance, muttering "There's nothing to read in it".

After all, your aim is more likely to be to communicate with others, rather than to sell them something. To this end, you will need to ensure that advertisements do not look the same as editorial, that one is clearly distinguished from the other. If the distinction looks like becoming blurred, since advertisements often copy editorial styles, then an advertisement should be labelled as such.

Small, or classified, adverts are the ones most likely to appear in a desktop publication, since it is likely to be aimed at a specialist audience such as collectors – of stamps, comic–books, false teeth or whatever – who will want to swop, or buy or sell collectables.

These should be grouped together on a page, with each advert set in a small box of a fixed size, probably one inch deep by a column across, two inches deep by a column across or three inches deep. The regularity of size makes them easy to fit into a page and the only problem is arranging the type within each box to look as attractive as possible.

You would need to fix a limit on the number of words that can fit into a box. An inch box will accommodate no more than 40. They should be set in a type a size or two smaller than the main body of the publication, which will probably mean in 8 point.

Display advertisements, occupying a larger space, will also need some kind of box or rule around them to mark them off from your editorial content. It might also be worth reserving some typefaces specifically for advertisements, thus signalling to the reader that they are not news or opinion. Use a lighter type–face for advertisements, reserving the heavier, bolder faces for your headlines and the balance will be better.

5.5 Decoration
While newsletters favour an austere approach, there is plenty of room for a more exuberant style in publications concerned with vigorous activities, from mountaineering to rock music. There is no good reason to ignore decorative typography, which can include fancy borders, elaborate drop capitals and even text surrounded by illustration, as was often the medieval

style. Decoration can add to the impact of posters or handbills, which may otherwise be disregarded, lost in the mass of such information that bombards us on all sides.

Ballads and broadsides that were hawked around the streets for three hundred or more years in Britain are known as "catchpenny prints" because that is precisely what they did, encouraging the passerby to part with money to satisfy his or her curiosity.

They can serve as models for posters in their popular use of big headlines and simple graphics to put across their message. A poster bearing a bold illustration, made more prominent by leaving white space around it, and an elaborate border, will attract the eye.

Title pages and frontispieces of books can also gain from a decorative treatment. They have disappeared from most books, having been replaced in appeal by the book jacket, which is a potent sales device. But they will retain their appeal long after book jackets have become creased and crumpled. Chapter titles also provided scope for decorative effect, particularly when combined with drop capitals.

5.6 Justification
Whatever you intend to produce with DTP software, from a personal letter to a technical manual, there are some basic decisions to be made and some important points to remember concerning the way type is placed on the page.

The most important involves justification of the text, that is setting the words so that they are flush with both the left– and the right–hand margins. It is the way most books, newspapers and magazines are set. In magazines and especially books, the justification is so subtle that you hardly notice it, except for the fact that all the lines are of the same length. In newspapers, it is frequently crude, with large gaps between words. Many of the words, too, are broken, or hyphenated, in order to fit the lines.

Justification is automatic with DTP software, as it is with any decent word processing software. The cheaper software does it crudely, in the same way that newspapers set by hot metal do, by shifting the words to fill the line. More expensive software achieves better–looking results by a mixture of proportional spacing, where different characters take up differing amounts of room on the line, and micro–justification, in which spaces are inserted between letters as well as between words. The amount of space that can be inserted can often be adjusted by the user.

What you need to ask yourself, is whether justification is important to you.

To justify or not to justify, that is the question. Whether it is better to space words so that all lines are the same length, or to set them with only the left hand margin flush and the right ragged. Unjustified text is easier to set and looks as good.	To justify or not to justify, that is the question. Whether it is better to space words so that all lines are the same length, or to set them with only the left hand margin flush and the right ragged. Unjustified text is easier to set and looks as good.

Figure 5.1: *Two different settings of text, both to the same measure. On the left, the text is justified, with all lines of the same length. On the right, it is set unjustified, with a ragged right hand margin. The unjustified text has been set without hyphens to break words between lines. The hyphenation of "easier" would have meant less of a gap in the penultimate line.*

Would you lose anything by having a flush left– and a ragged right–hand margin? There are local newspapers which set lines with ragged endings either because it is quicker to do so or their computerised equipment cannot handle justification.

If for some reason you wish to set your text in narrow columns, then a ragged margin can have benefits. It means that words, unless they are very long, will not be broken at the end of lines, which makes them much easier to read.

Because there are no ugly spaces between words narrow unjustified columns can look neater than justified ones. If you print narrow columns of text, containing no more than six or seven words, then many of the lines will be of the same length anyway. Test it out on your word processor and see for yourself.

Unjustified text needs rules between the columns so that there is a clear indication where one lines ends and another begins. You would probably not want to set unjustified lines in a book, where the longer lines of type are much easier to arrange neatly, but it is worth considering for a newsletter or a company report.

5.7 Hyphenation
Hyphenation, which is the breaking of words over two lines, can present problems when you use justified text, depending on the DTP software you are using. Some DTP packages hyphenate words automatically, although the process is memory–intensive and usually requires the use of a hard disk.

To justify or not to justify, that
is the question. Whether it is
better to space words so that
all lines are the same length, or
to set them with only the left
hand margin flush and the right
ragged. Unjustified text is
easier to set and looks as good.

To justify or not to justify, that
is the question. Whether it is
better to space words so that
all lines are the same length, or
to set them with only the left
hand margin flush and the right
ragged. Unjustified text is
easier to set and looks as good.

Figure 5.2: *Two other possible unjustified settings of text. On the left, it is set with each line centred on itself. On the right, it is set with a flush right and a ragged left margin. Such settings are best confined to captions, since neither is as easy to read as words set justified or with a ragged right margin.*

Other software can cope with soft hyphenation, where you indicate the point at which to break a word by putting a hyphen in it. If the word falls at the end of a line, then it will be broken at the indicated point.

Soft hyphenation is probably best dealt with after you have put the words on the page, providing your software reformats the text automatically after you make changes to it.

At the cheaper end, DTP software ignores hyphenation altogether and you will need to examine the text after it has been set to make sure that there are no ugly rivers of white space threading through the justified lines. If there are you will need to make changes, possibly by replacing a long word with a shorter one, in order to achieve a more professional appearance to the page.

5.8 Kerning

Kerning is to do with the spacing of type, in particular with the space between individual characters. A kern is that part of the type that extends beyond its main body and is seen at its most extreme on a italic f. The top and the tail of the letter occupies part of the space of adjoining letters.

In order to get over the problem of what happens when two italic "f"s are printed together, conventional type-setting uses ligatures, in which the letters are pre-set at the correct spacing apart. Kerning makes a great difference to the appearance of a document. For the spacing between many letters needs adjustment if they are not to look ugly. Lines should be set so that they give the appearance of regularity. But if they were actually set with precisely the same amount of space between each letter, they would look wrong.

The correct spacing can only be done with the eye. If it looks right, it is right. In lower-case text, letters and words should not be spaced widely apart. The space between words needs to be no more than that occupied by the letter "i".

Some DTP software offers automatic kerning, but this usually requires either a computer with a very large memory or a hard disk, as the program usually looks up the correct setting in a table which, by its nature, takes up a lot of RAM. Others allow the user to alter the distance between letters.

Figure 5.3: *The difference between unkerned and kerned letters. In the kerned example, on the right, the tail of the second letter is tucked under the body-space of the first.*

How much time you spend upon kerning will depend upon the importance of the publication which you are preparing. It obviously matters more for something intended to have a long life. The problem is with capital letters rather than lower-case ones. Letters such as A, J, L, O, P, Q, T, V, W and Y need to be set closer to other letters so that the white space between them and adjoining letters seems to be the same.

If you have an L followed by an A, it is possible that the letters will need setting a little further apart, since however close you get the A to the L, you are still left with a great deal of white space.

You also need to have the spacing correct between punctuation marks and text. A full-stop should be followed by a space, though that space should be less if followed by one of the problem capitals listed above.

There should also be a space following a colon or a semi-colon. A comma should be followed by the normal spacing.

You will need to decide on the style to be followed for marking paragraphs. The choice is betweeen indenting the first line of the paragraph and leaving a line space between one paragraph and the next. The former is certainly best for publications resembling newspapers or magazines, and is probably the better choice for most purposes. If the paragraph ends a letter short of the length of the line, then, if you are using justified lines, it is best to finish it flush right.

You also need to be aware of paragraphs ending with a short line at the bottom or top of the page. It results in an ugly and excessive amount of white space and should be avoided. You need at least three full lines at the top of a page or a column. To avoid it, you'll either need to add to the preceeding copy (or increase the space between the lines) or to cut it.

5.9 Leading
Leading, which takes its name from the time when thin strips of lead were inserted between the type-set lines, is the process of adding white space between lines of type and is usually done to make it easier to read, although on occasion it may be carried out to increase the amount of space the copy occupies.

Some leading is essential, if the text is to be legible. This is particularly true of type printed on a dot-matrix machine.

Usually leading of one point is sufficient for the main body of the text. Thus 8 point type leaded one point will occupy the same vertical space as 9 point. Typographers talk of this as "eight on nine point". If there is no leading then the type is described as being set solid.

The amount of leading will depend upon the font used and the length of the line. A bold-face type will look very black if set solid. Again, it is a matter of deciding what looks best to you. For type up to 12 point, which is as big as the body text should normally be, one point leading will usually be sufficient when setting the text in columns.

In books, where the type ranges the width of the page, then setting the text with two or three point leading between lines may be necessary. With a short text, then setting the text in 11 or 12 points with two points leading will increase its apparent length without detracting from its readability.

5.10 White space
Probably the most important aspect of layout is not the size of the headlines or the quality of the graphics, but something more intangible, something that you can see but not read or decipher: white space. Headlines and pictures and text all need to breathe, to have room in which to create their effect. This

Set with no leading:

Leading can change the appearance of a page. It adds more white space, which makes it easier for the reader to follow a line of text with his or her eyes. But too much leading between lines can make the words harder to read, since the amount of white space becomes a distraction.

Set with 1 point leading:

Leading can change the appearance of a page. It adds more white space, which makes it easier for the reader to follow a line of text with his or her eyes. But too much leading between lines can make the words harder to read, since the amount of white space becomes a distraction.

Set with 2 points leading:

Leading can change the appearance of a page. It adds more white space, which makes it easier for the reader to follow a line of text with his or her eyes. But too much leading between lines can make the words harder to read, since the amount of white space becomes a distraction.

Set with 3 points leading:

Leading can change the appearance of a page. It adds more white space, which makes it easier for the reader to follow a line of text with his or her eyes. But too much leading between lines can make the words harder to read, since the amount of white space becomes a distraction.

Set with 4 points leading:

Leading can change the appearance of a page. It adds more white space, which makes it easier for the reader to follow a line of text with his or her eyes. But too much leading between lines can make the words harder to read, since the amount of white space becomes a distraction.

Set with 2 points leading:

Leading can change the appearance of a page. It adds more white space, which makes it easier for the reader to follow a line of text with his or her eyes. But too much leading between lines can make the words harder to read.

Set with 4 points leading:

Leading can change the appearance of a page. It adds more white space, which makes it easier for the reader to follow a line of text with his or her eyes. But too much leading between lines can make the words harder to read.

Figure 5.4: *The difference that leading between the lines of text makes to its appearance on the page, letting in white space.*

depends on white space, the gaps between one line of a headline and another, and between it and the text.

Within the text, too, white space exists after short lines and between the end of one paragraph and the beginning of another. It is for this reason that paragraphs should be kept on the short side, which means around ten lines in length, when type is set in narrow columns. Ill-placed short lines (widows and orphans) can result in ugly white spaces on pages, something discussed in greater detail in the next chapter.

Chapter 6: Make-up

Your first consideration in planning any kind of publication will be to decide what type to use. The choice will depend upon your purpose, whether you are producing a poster, which will depend upon bold display type, or a newsletter where your needs will be more subtle.

Much research has been done on what makes typefaces legible, and investigations have been made also into the preferences of readers. (Those who want to know more should read Sir Cyril Burt's fascinating *A Psychological Study of Typography*, published by Cambridge University Press.)

The evidence is that readers are oblivious to the differences between one kind of typeface and another. They do not notice the form of the words, but only their content.

6.1 Choosing a typeface

Research has shown that, for the text, Roman typefaces are easier to read than sans serif ones. The reason is that lower-case letters are read by scanning the tops of the letters. A Roman face shows greater differentiation, and hence easier recognition, than a sans-serif one.

Which line is easier to read?

Which line is easier to read?

Figure 6.1: *We read the printed word by scanning the tops of letters. As the above settings of the question "Which line is easier to read?" demonstrate, the top line, set in a serif face, is easier to recognise than the sans-serif face below it. The reason is that the letters of the serif face are more clearly differentiated from each other, while the shapes of several of the letters of the sans-serif face are very similar to each other.*

The shapes of Roman letters, too, add a variety missing from the sometimes monotonous regularity of sans-serif fonts. Nevertheless, it is possible that you may decide that a sans-serif face would be more suitable for your purposes. A well-chosen sans-serif face is not hard to read and can provide a more approachable image. If your publication needs a modern feel about it then a sans–serif font such as the ubiquitous Helvetica will be more to your purpose, rather than the classicism that a Roman face would provide.

It is not necessary to have a great many typefaces in order to create an effective publication. You can get by with one, in different styles: 9 point for the body of text, together with 9 point italic, 12 point for important items or the first paragraphs to the main articles, and a larger size, 24 point, in bold for headings.

6.2 Headlines
Careful spacing of capital letters is the main requirement in setting headlines. In headlines that occupy more than one line, the sense should follow the lines. Words must never be broken between one line and another. Punctuation, too, is best avoided, unless it is essential, such as quotation marks around a remark. Use single quotes rather than double, and even then it is best to rewrite the headline to avoid their use.

Two American researchers, D. G. Paterson and M. A, Tinker reported in their book *How To Make Type Readable* (Harper and Row, 1940), that headlines in upper– and lower–case were easier to read than headlines that used only upper–case. Words in capitals took 12 per cent longer to understand.

There are two ways of setting headlines in upper– and lower case. You have a choice of beginning each word in the headline with a capital letter or of following the usual style in sentences where the first word and proper nouns are capitalised.

The second, presumably, is easier to understand, though I am not aware of any research into the two styles. As it follows normal practice, it is to be preferred, on the whole. Whichever you decide to use, remember to maintain the one style throughout any particular publication. If you mix styles, your readers will begin to wonder why some headlines have capital for every word and others do not. Stylistic consistency keeps readers happy.

You can mix upper–case headlines, which are probably best restricted to the main story, and upper– and lower–case headlines in the same publication or, indeed, on the same page. Sometimes, particularly when you want to draw attention to something, a short headline printed in capitals in large type will be most effective. Do keep such headlines really short, though. One word will suffice, if you can think of the right one.

Headlines, of course, can be set in many dazzling styles, in tinted boxes or in white letters reversed out of a black background, which is probably the only

GET IMPACT
INTO YOUR
HEADLINES

Get Impact
Into Your
Headlines

Get Impact
into your
Headlines

Get impact
into your
headlines

Figure 6.2: *Four styles of headline settings: all capital letters; capitals for the first letter of the words; a mixture of capitals and lower–case, according to the importance of the words; all lower–case apart from a capital for the first word and for proper nouns. Current practice favours the lower–case approach.*

time you should use such a style. Text that is white on black is very hard to read, even with the most expert typesetting. Current practice usually puts a headline or lines flush with the left–hand side of a column. As it is what people are used to, you might as well stick to the convention, unless you want to surprise readers.

The main headline on a page may well have a line above it, usually in a smaller typeface, which is known as the strapline. The strapline may also be set flush left or centered. It adds a little white space around the main headline as well as some extra information. Two headlines in the same typeface should not be positioned so that they are next to one another, an appearance that resembles tombstones.

Subheadings within the text are probably best set in a bold version of the body type. If you don't have one, you can always take the body type itself and enlarge it, something that most DTP packages will allow you to do.

Whether sub– or cross–headings are set centered or flush left is a matter of choice. They need to be set nearer the text that follows them, and to which they refer, than to the preceding text, so that there is more white space above than below them.

6.3 Captions
A graphic or any kind of illustration will need an explanatory caption. This are best set in a contrasting style to the face used for the body of the text,

| Add punch to your headings | 'ADD IMPACT' IS HIS GOOD ADVICE |

| Add punch to your page | Add extra impact to the page |

Figure 6.3: *Some different arrangement of headlines on the page. They can be set flush left, which is probably the most common style found today. Flush left headlines should be indented slightly from the edge of the column. If you use quotation marks in flush left settings, use single quotes and float them over the edge of the text so that the first letter of the next line is set flush with the first letter of the headline. Headlines can also be set with the lines centred, which works best when each line is shorter than the preceding one, as above. They can be set flush right, which is recommended only for occasional effects.*

such as the bold or the italic version of the body face. A caption positioned beneath an illustration looks neater when it is indented by a space at each end, but otherwise runs the length of the illustration.

If there is more than one line, then they should be of equal length, set to the same width. Captions to one side of an illustration should be set justified as a block of text. A short final line to a caption should be avoided.

6.4 Graphics
If the illustrations are of people, then they should be looking to the right on a left–hand page and to the left on a right hand page. Indeed, whatever the illustration, it should always lead the reader's eye into the page and not away from it.

6.5 Margins
The importance of white space in designing a page cannot be overestimated. It adds contrast and colour and gives the reader's eye somewhere to rest. A

A strapline with a subsidiary thought

ADD PUNCH TO YOUR STORIES

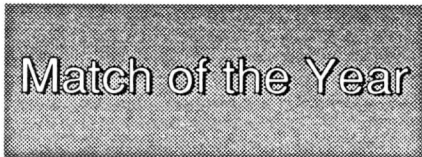

Figure 6.4: *Headline techniques. A strapline above a headline should be set in a contrasting style – upper– and lower–case if the main headline is capitals and vice versa – and is probably best centered on the main headline. Extra contrast can be added by setting headlines against tinted backgrounds. Desktop publishing also makes easy the superimposition of type so that unusual effects can be created.*

light and airy page looks more attractive than one dense with print. Margins, which are nothing but white space, play an important part in the look of a page. In magazines, margins tend to be the same width on each of the four sides of a page. But in a book the sizes of margins usually differ. The widest margin is at the bottom of the page. Then comes the margin on the paper's outside edge, then the margin at the top of the page, and the narrowest is the inside one.

How wide the margins are is a matter of personal taste and also depends on whether the book is to be printed conventionally or by laser printer or photocopier. In conventional printing, the paper will be trimmed and bound which will reduce the margin's sizes. The best way to work out the correct size is to find a book whose design you admire and measure it. You should allow at least 3 picas (half–an–inch) for the narrowest margin. In which case you would need 4 picas at the top of the page, six picas for the outside edge and eight picas at the bottom of the page. Wide margins, which do, of course, use up more paper, are especially effective in books.

6.6 Books
Researchers have considered the question of the right length of line for a book, the one that avoids being either too short and so disjointed to read, and

too long, and thus tiring for the eye. The conclusion reached was that a single line should contain between two or three lower-case alphabets in the typeface chosen, which gives a maximum of 78 characters including the spaces between words. Probably 60–65 characters a line would be ideal. Depending on your vocabulary and love of polysyllables, that gives you around ten words to a line.

You save nothing by setting lines longer, since you would then require to add more leading between the lines in order that the text should stay legible.

There is more to books, of course, than the text, for they are made up of many parts that require different typographical treatment.

These include, in the order in which they are encountered:

- Half title
- Title page
- Details of copyright and printing
- Dedication (if any)
- Acknowledgements (if any)
- Preface
- Contents
- Chapter Title and text
- Notes
- Appendices
- Index

Not all of these are necessary. The half title is a hangover from the days when books were not bound by the publisher and can be dispensed with so that the book begins with the title page, which provides an opportunity for decorative flourishes. On the back, or verso of the title page, is a page which gives the copyright notice and information about the printing. If there is a dedication, then it will be placed on the following right-hand page.

Then follows acknowledgements to those who helped in the preparation of the book and a preface, if written by a person other than the author. Otherwise the preface should follow the contents page.

The contents page should also be on a right-hand page and contains a list of the chapters of the book. If there are illustrations, then a list of them should follow.

The first chapter ought to begin on a right-hand page and then the text follows through. You will need to decide whether succeeding chapters ought to start on a new page or just run on. It looks better for a chapter to start on a new page and also gives scope, where needed, for elaborate chapter headings and other typographical extras, such as beginning each chapter with a drop capital.

Notes are usually placed at the end of each chapter or after the text of the book, which makes for easier setting than having notes at the foot of pages. They are usually set in a smaller size than the text itself.

The end matter, appendices and so forth, should follow the same setting as the rest of the book, apart from the index, which should be set a size or two down.

Each page needs a page number. This can be set at the top, or, preferably, at the bottom of the page, and it can be positioned where you feel it looks right – either centred or towards the edge of the page, where it can be most easily found.

It is customary to print the title of the book at the top of the left–hand pages and the name of the chapter at the top of the right–hand pages. Such running heads are not essential, but they are a useful guide for readers.

If, for some reason, you decide that the book would benefit from being printed in columns rather than pages of text, then it is best to treat the layout in the same fashion as newsletters, which are discussed below.

6.7 Newsletters and magazines

A newsletter can be defined as a sober magazine, something of a rather austere design, where the content is of primary importance. Magazines, on the other hand, can range from pop or science fiction fanzines to school magazines, comics or the means of community communications. They provide an opportunity to let rip with dazzling designs, slanting headlines, experimental graphics and unusual effects.

But the basic approach in both instances is virtually the same. Newsletters can be set in a similar style to a book, with pages of long lines of text. But most often they will be set in two or three or even more columns to a page. The width of the setting will influence such matters as the size of type and whether or not it is to be justified.

One task that DTP software has made virtually redundant is estimating the amount of copy you have and the amount needed to fill the space you have allowed. This is a process known as casting off, and requires complex calculations, first to discover the number of characters and then to discover, by using a type gauge, how much space a given typeface will occupy. It is calculated with typed manuscripts by working out the number of characters – letters and spaces – in an average line and then counting the lines.

Multiplying the two together gives you the number of characters in the manuscript. Dividing the total by six (the average length of a word in the English language) gives you the number of words. All you then need to establish is the number of words you can get in a typeset page and you will know the number of pages your publication requires.

Fortunately, many word processing programs provide a word or character count, which simplifies the calculations. But unless you are dealing with a very long manuscript, it is as quick to use DTP software to put the text into pages and see the number of pages it fills.

This is particularly easy to do with software that allows the text to flow from one column to the next automatically. For newsletters, it is much the best way. Once you have discovered how much space the text occupies, you can then know at once whether there are too many or too few words and how much space will be available for illustrations and headlines.

6.8 The modular approach

If you are producing a regular publication, then, once you have established a suitable layout, you can stick with it for every issue. If, such as with a parish, or community group magazine, it is covering the same kinds of activities with each issue, then these can be grouped together under the same label or logo each time.

Thus, once the basic shape of your publication is decided, it can retain it in all succeeding issues. Consistency is the easiest and quickest way of establishing an identity. It's also the neatest and quickest way of producing a issue after issue of a publication. It means that you can more or less pour the text into a mould each time, that you know how many words you require to fill each section and can cut or add as necessary.

Total inflexibility, of course, is not a good idea. You need to respond to changing circumstances, but within a carefully defined formula. How do you define that formula? A modular approach is the best, particularly for novices. It enables you to produce a layout that at least has the merit of neatness and order.

It is rather like building with bricks. Some bricks will be bigger than others, but their size will have a clearly defined relationship – they will be twice as deep as the others, or twice as deep and twice as wide, and so on and so forth. With a modular approach, you layout the space as a series of rectangles that either run across the page or down it. The headline and illustration, if any, is confined within the rectangle. Horizontally, the module is defined by the number of columns you have. Vertically, you can divide the page as you like, but, given the limitations of an A4 page and for the sake of simplicity, it is enough to divide it into three equal parts.

Within that grid, you can then fit your copy. There is a great deal of flexibility, particularly with a three column layout. For example, within the top third of the page, you could have a headline that ran across the three columns over a two column story and a one column illustration, or have the headline over one column story with a two column illustration, or put the headline down the first column, with the story occupying the next two columns. Stories and illustrations, of course, can occupy two–thirds or even the whole of the page.

You have a choice of designing a page that is mainly vertical, with the stories running from top to bottom, or mainly horizontal, with the stories running across the page, or a mixture of both, with, say, a horizontal box in the top third of the page and then the stories underneath it running down the page.

Virtually all the professional designers of British publications produce mainly vertical layouts and, as a result, that is what readers are used to and thus prefer. But horizontal designs can look attractive. They have an orderly quality that can be most effective when allied to the right kind of publication – they wouldn't work for a punk rock fanzine, say, but would project an image of calm and tidiness that could be of an advantage to a parish magazine.

The size of a particular rectangle or square on the page will be dependent upon the amount of copy and the illustration. If it's a short item there is no problem. It goes down a single column with a single column headline over it and another short item or two, similarly treated beneath it. If these fall short of the available space it takes no great ingenuity to add a line to one of the headlines.

A larger block can be trickier, although the same principles apply. You can increase the size of the illustration, if there is one, or bump up the size of the headline or add some decorative flourish – a box around the copy, or a thick rule under it may be enough to make the text fill the alloted space.

This minor juggling, anyway, is far easier to do than the complex jigsaw of a more unstructured layout, where you let the copy run down from one column to the next until it ends, and then search around for something to fill the odd-shaped hole it leaves on the page.

It makes sense to begin your publication at the beginning: with the front page. If it's a poster-styled page, the equivalent of a magazine cover, then you can probably design it on-screen, without recourse to pencil and paper. It is this ability to shift things around, and see them as they will be printed, that gives desktop publishing an advantage over more conventional methods.

A poster cover is simple. Put the title of the publication at the top and use bold text to indicate the contents. If you've bold pictures, remembering that large-scale illustrations can look tatty when produced on a dot-matrix printer, then so much the better. Conventionally, it's necessary to plan the layout in detail on paper, or even, in publications where deadlines are not urgent, to manipulate the illustrations and the headline text by shifting them around under a transparent layout sheet. With desktop publishing, all the manipulation can be done on screen. Even so, a rough sketch on paper can provide a useful aid.

If your publication's front page is going to look more like a mini-newspaper, then you'll begin by laying out the main story. You'll need to know, before you begin, the number of words contained in the story.

If you use a wordprocessor to prepare the text, which is far the best way, you may well have a word-count, which divided by the number of words you can get in a line, will give you a good enough idea. If your word processor doesn't give you a word count (an essential too many word-processing programmers ignore), then it might be worth printing the text at a character setting that is the same as your column width. You can then put the printed text on the paper and get a precise reading of the space it will fill.

If the story is accompanied by an illustration, you will now have to decide how much space that will occupy. Is it to go across one, two or three columns? If it's at a large size, will it leave the space you need for the text? Is the image as you want it, or should it be made bigger? Smaller? Would it be improved by cropping, to make the image tighter? Or should it be made bolder, by cropping and enlarging? With desktop publishing, you can manipulate the image instantaneously and discover what effects you can create.

You'll also need to consider the headlines and what type are most appropriate for them. And you'll also need to consider what other stories and illustrations you want to put on your front page and how much space they will occupy. Because of the limitations of an A4 page, it is best not to try to

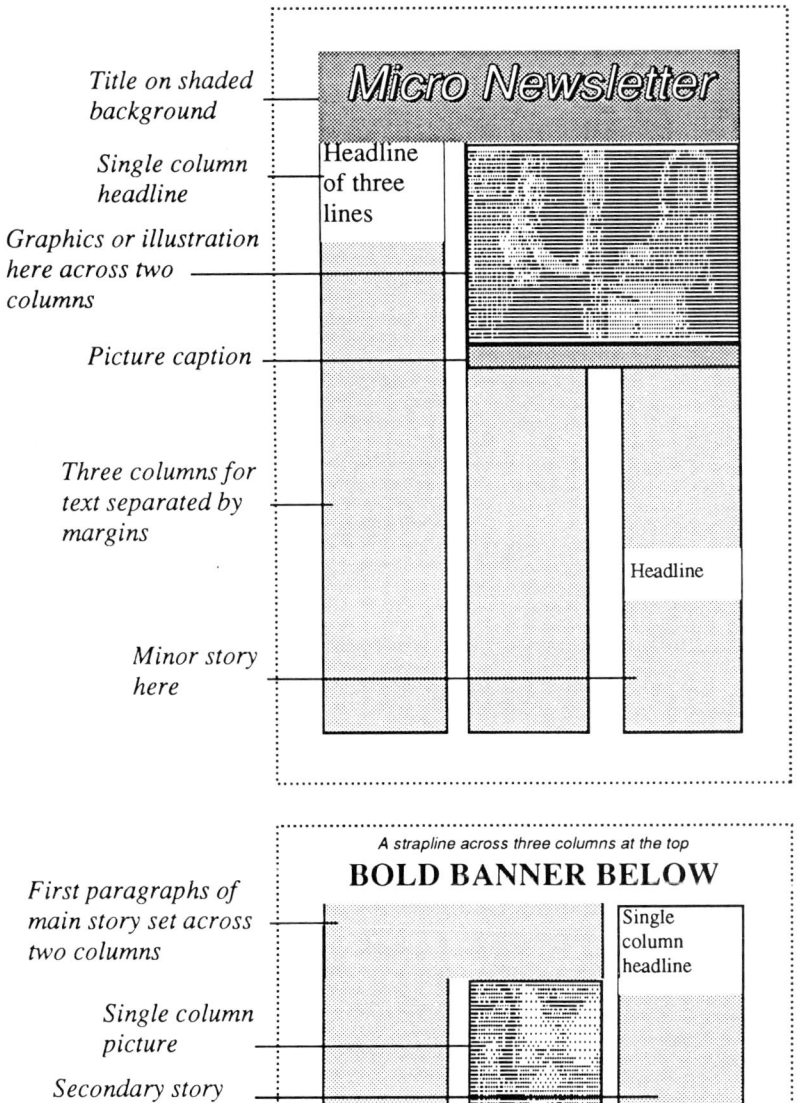

Figure 6.5: *Top, a suggested three column layout for an A4−sized newsletter, which would provide three columns of text set at 14.5 picas. Below it is a different treatment for the top half of the page, as a variation on the same modular layout, with a banner headline and a single column illustration.*

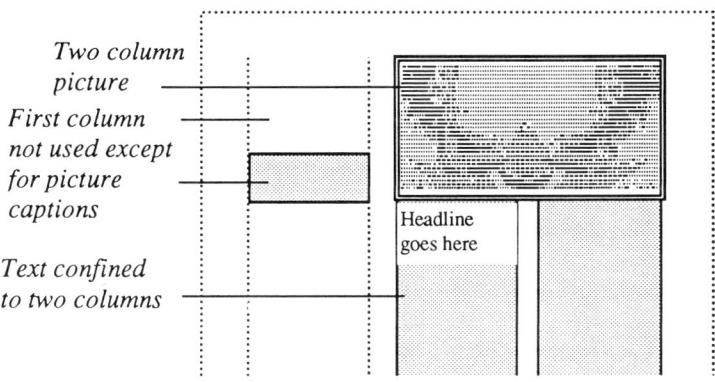

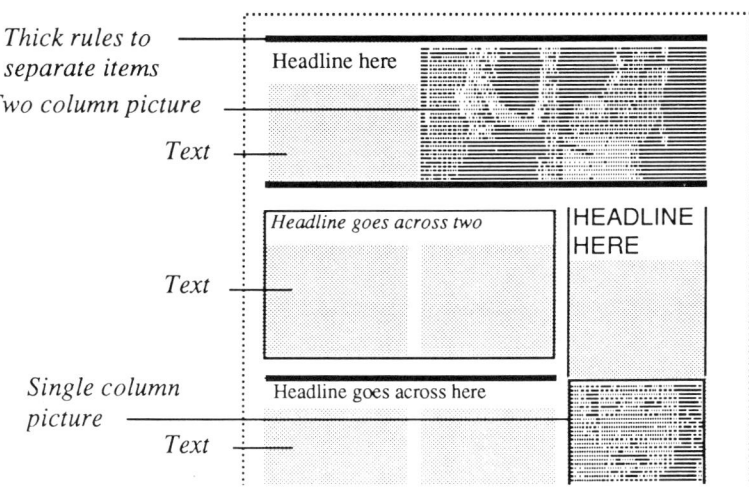

Figure 6.6: *Two further variations on layout with the three column grid. In the top example only two columns are used for text. The first column is used only for picture captions. This asymetric approach gives a modern look to a page, although it uses more paper. Below it is an example of a design based on a horizontal grid, with most stories running across the page rather than down it. One result of such an approach is that individual items have less space than they would with a layout where they ran down the page. If you have to publish many shortish items, it is a stylish way to deal with them.*

73

cram too much into it. A main story and a subsidiary one or a panel giving an indication of the contents of the rest of the publication will probably be enough.

6.9 A4 layout

There are three styles of layout most suitable for an A4 page. You can use a poster style, which requires a single column format, or use two or three columns. It is possible to have more than three columns, but not advisable. Four columns or more provide a very narrow measure, which means that the text is harder to read and the problems of justification and the hyphenation of words are greater. Of the three approaches, the three column one provides the greatest flexibility, particularly when integrating words and pictures.

Layout, of course, is dependent upon the purpose of the publication. For a newsletter, or a newspaper in miniature, three columns is probably best. But if you want the less strident approach of a magazine, then two columns may be preferable. For, say, a poet, a single column will be the ideal, but a single column surrounded by plenty of white space, which in practice can mean using a three column layout, but using only the centre column, with the two outside ones transformed into wide margins.

If you intend to produce a regular publication, then you need to think out its form in advance, since it should be recognisably the same publication from one issue to the next (unless, of course, its function is to demonstrate different approaches).

Having once formulated your front page, then stick with that design – even if you decide it could be improved – for some appreciable time. Readers do not like sudden changes. For the same reason, the general format should remain the same unless there is a pressing reason for making alterations. This is an aid not only to readers, but to yourself.

Once the format is decided and regular features introduced, whether it be letters from readers or reports of Women's Institute meetings, then the publication becomes far easier to produce. You will quickly discover how many words will fit into a column or a page, you will be able to use the same headings or logos each time, which means that they only have to be set or drawn once, and you will be publishing something that acquires its own lasting instantly indentifiable character.

You will also need to consider at an early stage precisely how your publication is to be printed, whether it is going to be run off on your printer, which inevitably will be a slow and tedious process if you have more than half−a−dozen to produce, or whether it will be photocopied, which is the best of the cheaper alternatives, or printed conventionally. Obviously, if you use a dot–matrix printer to produce all your copies then the paper will be printed on one side only. But if you use other methods, then it is likely that you'll print on both sides of the paper, as with commercial magazines.

6.10 The double page spread
If you print on both sides of the paper, then you need to remember that it is the two pages – a double–page spread – that needs to be treated as the unit of design.

The two can form part of the same feature and be linked in some way, by a headline that goes across both pages. Or it may be that the writing carries across from one page to the next. Or, indeed, they may be concerned with different matters. But whatever the situation, you need to be aware of what is on each page so that they form a harmonious whole and do not cancel each other out.

The obvious way to create harmony is to make each page a mirror image of the other, at least in the first stages of layout. You can then make shifts of emphasis knowing at least that the balance is right.

A three column layout is more flexible, and, as a result, harder to use effectively. It requires greater skill and forethought, although the result can look better. The extra flexibility is particularly useful in dealing with illustrations, since a picture can be a single column, a double column or across all three columns. Thus it is best suited for publications with a high graphic content. If your taste runs to words rather than pictures, then a two column format is probably more suitable.

6.11 Two column layout
In a two column magazine–style format, the opening page of any piece of writing that occupies more than one page will probably follow a simple, fairly standard format. Such a page divides fairly naturally into three more or less equal portions. In the top third of the page will be some form of illustration – a picture or some graphic, such as a map or a diagram – that relates to the article.

Below that comes the headline – a single line of upper– and lower–case across the two columns. Then a by–line, giving the name of the author. Then a standfirst, which is two or three lines explaining the article and providing the reader with reasons and encouragement to read it.

A standfirst is the printed equivalent of a fairground barker, trying to attract customers to *his* or *her* sideshow: "Everything you wanted to know about sex and royalty, by a man who has an intimate relationship with both" is an example of a standfirst that might have many reading on (though I'm not sure whether such a feature could fill a page.)

The standfirst is probably best set in a larger version of the typeface used for the main text, which is easy enough to do. Simply set the lines in the typeface you intend to use for the text and then make it twice the size.

If the main text is being set justified, then it may be worthwhile setting the standfirst unjustified. This is a simple way of adding a little white space, which can improve the appearance of the opening. After that you begin the feature proper.

You need some sign to indicate the start, either by using a drop or decorated capital letter for the first word or by some other typographical signal such as a black block or star on the first line, followed by setting the first two or three words in capital letters.

The text would then run down the first column and then down the second and over to the next page. It is possible to have pages that consist entirely of text, but it is better in such cases to have more than one story on a page to add the contrast of headlines and possibly another typestyle.

If you are using a dot–matrix printer, then the quality of print is not good enough for you to be able to get away with a page of unadorned text. In order to achieve a more attractive layout you can continue the main story down the first column of the page, turning into the second column.

Then you fill the rest of the second column with a short item of information that will occupy the remainder of the column. You set it within a box, which can be plain or with a decorative border. You give it a two–line headline, which can be set inverted – white letters on a black or a shaded background – to emphasise its difference. And you can also set the text in a different typeface as a further contrast. If the main story is long, then it can turn on to the next page.

An alternative design is to put another story at the bottom of the page across the two columns. with the main story doubling up above it. A single line for a headline will probably suffice, and again the body of the text can be set in a contrasting typeface. A shallow space, not more than six or seven lines deep is all that is needed to add interest and diversity to the page.

This basic layout will serve throughout the magazine, with the longer articles running round the shorter items. To avoid monotony, the layout can be varied without altering the basic structure. For example, you can run the standfirst above the main headline rather than below it. And you can put the shorter items at the top of the page rather than at the bottom. Extra variety can be added by setting the short items across the two columns rather than keeping to the usual two single-column settings.

There are other ways of ringing the changes, such as setting the headline and standfirst in one column of a double column page and putting the text in the second column, a sort of asymmetrical approach that can look very effective, provided it is not done too often.

Long text needs to be broken up by cross-heads, small single-line headlines of one, two or three words that usually convey very little information but provide a contrast and add some white space.

Like a standfirst, crossheads are probably best set in a larger version of the body-type. They can be set centered on the line, with space above and below them. Or they can be set as the first words of a paragraph, in which case

Cross-headings need to be set closer to the text that follows them than to the text in the preceding paragraph.

Shock horror

You need to pick out the word for the heading from nearby text. It helps if these include shock or horror or an emotive word.

Cross-headings need to be set closer to the text that follows them than to the text in the preceding paragraph.

Cross-headings need to be set closer to the text that follows them than to the words that come before.

Horror shock

You need to pick out the word for the heading from nearby text. It helps if these include shock or horror or an emotive word.

Cross-headings need to be set closer to the text that follows them than to the words that come before.

* * * * * * * * *

You need to pick out the word for the heading from nearby text. It helps if these include shock or horror or an emotive word.

Cross-headings need to be set closer to the text that follows.

Horror shock

You need to pick out the word for the heading from nearby text. It helps if these include shock or horror or an emotive word.

Figure 6.7: *Different styles for setting cross-headings, which can be replaced by such graphical means as stars. Their main purpose is to add white space to the page.*

they will have to be the same size as the body text. In order to make them stand out, you will need to set them in a bolder typeface. Such headings should be set with more space above them than below them so that it is closer to the body text to which it refers.

If you want to produce publications of a larger size, then it is simplest to revert to old fashioned methods of make-up, involving scissors and paste.

Part Four
Mainly hardware

Chapter 7: Printers

Printing is the weakest part of desktop publishing. The problem is not so much one of quality, as of speed. The quality is not as good as conventional typesetting, of course, but often that does not matter. Much printed matter is ephemeral: read today, thrown away tomorrow. So long as it serves its purpose and can be read without difficulty, a publication does not need to try to match the highest standards. Even the output from dot-matrix printers can be perfectly acceptable in many circumstances.

But speed is of the essence. The fastest laser printer, can manage around 15 pages a minute, which is simply too slow to produce a long publication. In everyday use, its output is much slower, particularly if it is processing many pages containing graphics.

In extreme cases, a laser printer may sit there for twenty minutes while constructing an image of complex graphics before it begins to print it. On the other hand, once one copy of a page of mainly text has been made, a laser printer will run off further copies in a matter of seconds.

A dot-matrix printer, in its bit-mapped graphics mode, will take five minutes or more to print a single page and there is no saving in speed on further pages. You could grow old waiting for it to finish more than one copy of any publication.

If you need only one or two copies, then the speed is bearable. Otherwise, you will use a computer printer only to make a master copy of a publication. This can then be photocopied to run off a few more, or it can be printed in a conventional manner by photocomposition, which involves making an image on film of the finished page, making a printing plate from that and printing it, probably using web-offset methods.

The advantage of photocomposition is that the result will look like a conventional piece of printing to the unpractised eye. It won't be as good since a master copy produced on a laser or a dot-matrix printer will be inferior, though much cheaper, than conventionally typeset copy. The quality can be measured in dots per inch (dpi), which provides an indication of the density of the printing. Conventional methods result in at least 1200 dpi.

A laser can manage 300 dpi, although printers capable of higher resolutions are likely to appear very soon. Dot-matrix printers vary from around 90 dpi to resolutions that come close to laser printers. An alternative to using a

Printers

printer driven by your microcomputer is to have the copy typeset in the traditional way from the document stored on your floppy disk, a subject which is dealt with in the next chapter.

Another is to link the computer to a phototypesetting machine directly instead of to a laser printer. Packages such as Aldus's *PageMaker* and Xerox's *Ventura Publisher* can drive typesetting machines like Linotype's Linotronic 100 or 300, with resolutions of 1270 dpi and 2540 dpi respectively. Indeed, if your DTP software is *PostScript* compatible (an explanation of *PostScript* will be found later in this chapter), or possibly even if it is not, then it can be linked to typesetters.

7.1 Types of printer

Printing technology is changing fast and it may well be that someone will soon invent a cheaper and quicker method than those currently available, thus freeing desktop publishing from the last of its limitations.

At the moment, you have a choice between using four different kinds of printer:

- Laser
- Dot–matrix
- Ink jet
- Daisywheel.

A laser printer gives the best results. A dot–matrix printer can produce acceptable results on the level of parish magazines and is useful for producing page proofs before you commit yourself to producing the master copy with the laser printer, which is far more expensive to run. An ink jet produces results similar to a dot–matrix, is quieter, but messier and of little advantage unless you want to print in not very good quality colour.

It is possible to find a colour printer that matches the quality of laser printing. Mitsubishi's colour thermal printer G650 has a resolution of 300 dpi. But it is extremely expensive. If you want colour in desktop publishing, it is better to revert to traditional methods of adding them at the printing stage in the conventional way.

Dot–matrix and laser printers work directly with desktop publishing software, since they are capable of reproducing graphics. A daisywheel printer cannot normally be linked to such software, since it resembles an electric typewriter. There is one DTP package, Savtek's *ETG Integrated Word Processing and Graphics Desktop Publishing System* for the IBM PC, that permits the use of a daisy–wheel, using the full–stop to produce graphics. Its speed, as you can imagine, is slow.

A daisywheel does produce very good quality print and can be used, in conjunction with a word processor, to type the body–text of a document, which can then be pasted–up to be printed conventionally. More about the use of daisywheels can be found in the next chapter.

7.2 Laser printers

A laser printer looks and, to a casual onlooker, works much like a photocopier. Blank paper goes in one side and comes out the other printed. It uses a similar technology, so much so that there is at least one laser printer, produced by Canon, that also doubles as a photocopier.

Its obvious difference from other computer–controlled printers is that it does not print a page sequentially, line by line, but prints it all at the same time, which is why such machines are also known as page printers.

It was the advent of laser printers for personal computers in 1985 that made desktop publishing possible. The first laser printers had appeared a few years before, worked with mini– or mainframe computers, were capable of printing text only and cost hundreds of thousands of pounds.

The technology is not only new, it is changing rapidly. Already laser printers are half the price and twice the speed of what they were when they were launched. It should not be long before they are easily affordable by individuals as well as businesses.

For any business that produces printed matter, a laser printer is an excellent investment and will quickly save far more than its cost. There are around 30 different models on the market. Apart from the brand name, many are otherwise the same, built from almost identical components. Several use the Canon printing engine, for instance.

A laser printer roughly resembles the way an offset printer works, in that an image is transferred first to a roller and then to paper that passes under the roller. It is a specialised computer, often using the same 68000 microprocessor found in Atari ST, Commodore Amiga and Macintosh computers, and is likely to have a memory larger than the personal micro to which it is linked. It needs this capacity in order to construct within it an image of the page to be printed.

The hard work of creating the image is done by a raster–image processor (RIP), which builds the picture in much the same way as is done on a monochrome television set, forming it a dot at a time from a sequence of black and white dots. The image is then transferred by means of a laser beam to an electrically charged photo–sensitive drum, which develops a charge wherever the beam touches it.

Then a toner, an electrostatic black powder as used in photocopiers, adheres to the image created by the laser scan. The paper passes under the drum and the powdered image is impressed upon it. Heat under pressure is applied – and the paper emerges, bearing the final black and white print.

Laser printers can be used in two ways: as a glorified dot–matrix printer producing hard copy of your finished page as you see it on the screen, or as a printer controlled by a page description language and using built–in fonts to produce work that looks, at a cursory glance, as if it has been printed by conventional means.

In its dot–matrix style, it will produce a higher quality of output than an ordinary dot–matrix, matching the so–called "letter quality" of the best daisywheel printers. But, bit–mapped graphics will suffer from the same problems as any other dot–matrix print–out: there will be visible steps in curves and slanting lines so that the result will have a visible roughness.

Laser printers used in this way tend to be compatible with the printing codes used by IBM or Epson dot–matrix printers. The problems with dotty print are eliminated when the laser printer is controlled by a page description language rather than reproducing the screen display. But you have to pay for quality.

A laser printer used with a page description language needs an extremely large memory. To process an A4 page of graphics requires a minimum of 1Mbyte memory, as a quick calculation will reveal. An A4 page has an area of 96.68 square inches. A laser printer has a resolution of 90,000 dots per square inch, giving a total of around 8,710,000 dots. Each dot requires one bit in memory to represent it.

Additional memory is required to store and manipulate fonts, so that at least 1.5Mbytes is needed for the best results. As the resolution of laser printers is improved and as the size increases of paper on which they can print, so their memory requirements will grow correspondingly.

An alternative approach has been taken by Atari, which is to manufacture a low–cost laser printer that uses the 2Mbyte or 4Mbyte memory and 68000 microprocessor of its Mega ST computers to control the printing process. The savings in cost need to be weighed against the fact that the computer cannot be used for any other purpose as long as printing continues, although the use of any laser printer is likely to occupy any computer for long periods.

Some printers are limited in the size of type that they can print. There are laser printers that can manage only 12 point type, which is extremely restricting. For successful desktop publishing, you need to use fonts up to at least 24 or 36 points and for some purposes, such as the production of posters, you need type up to 72 points in size. There are also restrictions on the number of different fonts that can be used on a page, although most can manage an adequate number. There is little advantage in mixing a great number of fonts on a page, except for some very special and unusual use, such as setting a headline with every letter in a different font or style.

In order to change fonts, some machines make use of plug-in cartridges, which can be fiddly in use. Running costs of laser printers are also high, averaging about 4p a page. Maintenance can be expensive. The toner may need replacing every 3,000 pages. In some printers, the toner and drum cartridge is replaced at the same time; in others, the drum will last for around 10,000 pages and the toner even longer.

There are limitations in the size of paper a laser printer can handle. Most can cope with A4, but few of them can manage A3 and those that do are extremely expensive. Some early models have a small paper tray, capable of holding no more than 100 sheets, so that it needs frequent re-filling.

Apple's LaserWriter, which is sold with Macintosh desktop publishing systems, is obviously best suited for use with the Mac and has fewer limitations than most. It is possible to link a LaserWriter to other computers, including the IBM PC and the Commodore Amiga. The LaserWriter has 1.5 Mbytes of memory and another 512K that is used as a permanent store for fonts (it has as standard Courier, Helvetica and Times Roman), and the page description language *PostScript*. Its typefaces can be printed at any size from 4 point to 720 point, which is 10 inches high, since the printer can automatically re-size them from the one font held in memory.

Hewlett-Packard's LaserJet was the first low-cost laser printer, but suffered from its inability to produce large graphics because of the limitations of its memory. The LaserJet Plus has overcome these problems and many DTP programs include printer drivers for it.

7.3 Page description languages

Laser printers achieve excellent results when they are driven by as a page description language (or PDL for short). The best known of these is *PostScript*, endorsed by Apple and IBM. There are rivals, such as Xerox's

Figure 7.1: *An example of the way you can manipulate images using* PostScript, *reducing the size of the original pages and turning them at an angle. Producing a complex image such as this is a slow process. Using an Apple LaserWriter, it took more than 15 minutes to print.*

Interpress and *DDL (Document Description Language)*, which Hewlett–Packard has announced that it will support on its new machines, although it has added that it will also support *PostScript*. Thus *PostScript* is the nearest thing to a standard PDL for desktop publishing on personal computers.

Not all laser printers are *PostScript* compatible, but the majority seem to be, and it makes sense to use one that is, if you can afford to do so. *PostScript* has its limitations. *The Seybold Report*, the leading US newsletter of electronic publishing, reported recently that a map of the United States had taken 13 hours to typeset using *PostScript*. But, at the moment, it is the best there is and the one supported by most software.

More and more software is being issued in *PostScript* compatible forms, including at least 15 word processing programs – *GEM Write*, Microsoft's *Word, Samna Word III, WordPerfect* and *WordStar 2000* are among them – as well as graphics programs, including *Cricket Draw* for the Macintosh and programs that run under *GEM*, and integrated programs such as Lotus's *Jazz* and Microsoft's *Excel*.

At least fifty desktop publishing and typesetting programs (yes, I'm afraid there are that many), running on either the IBM PC and compatibles or the Macintosh are also *PostScript* compatible. In all, more than 200 software packages support it.

A page description language does what you would expect: it describes the page to the laser printer, telling it what stored fonts to use or sending a description of the fonts, perhaps as a bit map, and explaining what is to go where.

This activity is invisible to the user, since the DTP software translates the on–screen page you have designed into PDL code. The code is then sent to the printer where it is translated into a form that the RIP can use to command the laser beam to be switched on and off.

You can program directly in *PostScript*, if you so wish. Some DTP programs allow you access to the *PostScript* code they generate so that you can make changes to improve the printed result. Using *PostScript*, you can reduce, enlarge, stretch, compress, rotate and move text and graphics. The *PostScript* code for pages can easily be transferred from one computer to another, either by direct connection or over the telephone, using a modem.

7.4 Dot–matrix printers
There are around 200 dot–matrix machines on the market, making them the work–horses of computer printing. They are usually reliable and can print

both text and graphics so that they are the most popular, as well as the cheapest, printers and have managed to fight off the challenge both of daisywheel and inkjet printers. Whether they will be able to resist laser printers as well depends on how quickly laser printers fall in price.

The printing quality of dot—matrixes has improved dramatically in the last few months. The greatest disadvantage is the noise they produce. Lasers hum and occasionally whine, inkjets whisper, daisywheels clack away like typewriters, but dot—matrix printers whine and howl, buzz and grate. Fortunately, it is possible to buy acoustic hoods to keep down the noise.

They can print at high speeds, except when being used for desktop publishing. They work in a simple enough way. The machine's moving print—head contains wires, or pins, which hammer against a ribbon to produce a pattern, or matrix, of dots on the paper.

Recent dot—matrix printers tend to have at least two printing modes: draft and NLQ, for near—letter quality. In draft mode the head moves quickly across the paper, producing characters that are obviously made of dots and often ugly in appearance.

In NLQ mode the head makes several passes across the paper, moving a fraction each time so that the dots become denser. In this way, recognisable typefaces are printed that resemble the output of a daisywheel.

It is simple, too, to get such printers to print in several different styles: condensed, bold, enlarged and italic. Many offer a wide range of typefaces. Dot—matrix printers are fast, except when used for printing graphics, when the speed is similar to NLQ mode. In the beginning, the printers used nine pins in the print head. The resolution was around 90 x 120 dpi, although this was increased by the use of the NLQ mode.

Printers are now available with 18 or 24 pin printheads. The improvement in quality has been dramatic. Some 24 pin printers have a resolution of 360 x 180 dpi, which approaches the standard of laser printers. The result lacks the crispness of laser printer output, since the characters are not always perfectly aligned, as they cannot be when printed by a head moving across the paper. But it is good enough for many purposes.

There are dot—matrix machines, such as Apple's Imagewriter II, that print in colour, providing the software incorporates a suitable screen—dump program. Usually, it is simply a matter of substituting a four—colour ribbon for a monochrome one. With its range of 140 colours, the Imagewriter is better than most rivals, which tend to turn out muddy prints or ones in which the colours bear little resemblance to the original. Used for desktop publishing, dot—matrix printers can produce good enough results, particularly for non-professional purposes or for printed matter designed to have a brief life.

The final result will depend upon the software as much as the hardware. A 24 pin dot—matrix printer will show no improvement in quality over a nine pin printer when used with software written for a nine pin. The standard of dot-matrix drivers varies with different DTP packages. The best is to be found on *Publishing Partner* for the Atari ST, which produces excellent quality from a 24 pin machine.

Even if you use a laser printer, a dot—matrix is useful for providing a draft copy of your publication, so that you can check everything is as it ought to be, providing that the publication is not too long and you have time to spare.

7.5 Inkjet printers
Inkjet printers seem to me to have only one advantage over dot—matrix machines: they are much quieter. But some require special paper, can be messy to use and cost more to run than dot—matrix printers. The technology is similar, except that instead of pins hitting a ribbon, ink is squirted or vibrated from nozzles onto the paper. Inkjets are more acceptable as a means of producing colour printing. If you have DTP software that can handle colour and you want to run off a few—eye catching posters, then a colour inkjet is ideal and will provide a better quality output than a colour dot-matrix.

Among inexpensive colour printers Canon's PJ—1080A inkjet outperforms comparable dot—matrix printers and gives good results. If you have more money to spend, then Xerox's 4024 colour printer is worth considering.

7.6 Thermal printers
Thermal printers form another variation on the matrix approach. Most use a head containing wires which are heated and press against a special ribbon, melting the ink and forming an impression on the paper.

An exception is the IBM Quietwriter, which heats the ribbon itself. There are 40 electrodes in the head which form the pattern of the character when pressed against the ribbon, which contains heat—generating layers. The result is quiet, slow letter—quality printing which can use a variety of different fonts and so provide an alternative to a daisywheel.

Thermal colour printers use a four colour ribbon that will yield around a dozen prints before it will need replacing. They require special paper and tend to be extremely slow when used to print graphics. You can wait around a quarter of an hour for it to print a page. Colour printing is obviously going to become more important as desktop publishing moves away from monochrome, but at the moment the results are often unsatisfactory and the situation may be slow to imrpove.

7.7 Linotronic machines

Linotype's Linotronic 100 and 300 are typesetters which are *PostScript* compatible. That means that anything you can produce on a dot–matrix or laser printer, using one of the many *PostScript* compatible DTP packages, can be reproduced in high quality type by these machines. The 100 has a print quality of 1270 dpi and the 300 of 2540 dpi.

7.8 Photocopiers

Photocopiers, which are much faster than laser printers, can be used as a method of printing a completed publication. The latest photocopiers, which can usually be found in the many instant print shops in towns and cities, can reproduce photographs well and can collate and bind the printed pages.

Photocopiers can also enlarge or reduce the page size of a document. Enlarging can be used to produce a poster. Reduction can improve the apparent quality of the print, although you will have needed to take into consideration the size of type used on your master copy; making it smaller could affect its legibility. Photocopying is only worth considering for printing a small number of copies. For longer runs, more conventional methods are likely to be cheaper.

7.9 Duplicating machines

The cheapest method of printing is to use a duplicating machine and a stencil cut on a dot–matrix printer. The quality matches the cost, but it will be acceptable for some purposes.

It is also the cheapest way to add colour for a title or headline. You can cut a master containing only the title or headline, duplicate it using coloured ink, cut a master copy of the rest of the publication and then duplicate that on the paper containing the title or headline.

In order to cut a stencil you will need to remove the ribbon from your printer first. You will also need to check after cutting that there is no wax clogging the pins on the printhead. If there is, clean it carefully with a solvent.

Chapter 8: D–I–Y

Desktop publishing can be done without specialised software or expensive laser printers. It is just harder. On the other hand, you may find that using scissors and paste, together with a word processor and a printer, is more flexible. You are not constrained by the limitations of the software. You can produce a publication or a poster on whatever scale you like.

Even if you use DTP software, there will be times when a scissors and paste approach will be best, especially to overcome the problem of page size. You might want to produce a broadsheet newspaper, for instance. A daisywheel printer then comes into its own. The advantage of daisywheel printers is that the quality is excellent and the choice of typefaces is wide. You can obtain proportional print, in which letters take up a varying amount of space according to their size, rather than the standard typewriter approach where each letter, whether it is an "i" or an "m" occupy the same space.

You will have to sketch a rough layout, using the same modular approach described in the chapters on design. If you are producing a publication using multiple columns, then you simply decide the number of columns you want and set your word processor to produce a printout in a narrow measure. You need to remember to leave a gap between columns.

How easy it will be to get the measure right depends upon the sophistication of your word–processing software. If it provides rulers you will be able to set them to the correct measure. Otherwise, you will need to experiment by printing a line, counting the number of characters that fit into your measure and then setting the margins to that number.

Once the copy is printed, it is then simply a matter of cutting it to the required length with a pair of scissors and sticking it in position. It is best to use a petroleum–based glue such as Cow Gum since you can then slide the paper into position. If you have stuck it down on the skew, you will be able to pull it off the paper and stick it down again. If you are fearful of tearing the paper, then a squirt of lighter fluid will dissolve the gum. But it doesn't matter that much if you do make mistakes, since it is easy enough to print out a fresh copy of a column you have messed up. Illustrations can either be generated on the computer and stuck into position, or drawn. You can easily add photographs.

The master copy can then be photocopied, if the print run is small enough, or printed by means of photocomposition. The scissors and paste approach can be the best way to get a good quality master using a dot–matrix printer. One of the problems with low–cost DTP packages is that the quality of its body-text is mediocre.

It is not easy to design a small bit–mapped font that prints well. The preference is for sans serif faces, but these tend to be heavy and offer little encouragement to readers. An alternative is to use either a dot–matrix printer's NLQ quality print or to use one of the many print enhancement programs that enable a variety of typefaces to be produced from a dot–matrix printer.

Even if you are using a DTP software, there are advantages to be gained by dividing your task into two stages. First design the page, or pages, on-screen, making sure that the text, which should have been prepared with a word processing program, fits the available space. Include what computer-generated graphics you want and put them into position on the page.

Then remove the text from the pages, apart from the captions to the illustrations and the rules between columns if you are using them. Captions can be difficult to place manually, particularly if they are overlaid on the graphics, and a line or two in a hard–to–read typeface is no incentive to potential readers. The rules will provide useful guidelines for the final stage.

Next print the pages, which will be blank apart from the graphics and rules. Then print the text using a daisywheel or a dot–matrix's NLQ option at the correct column measure from your word processor. You may have to experiment here to discover which font from your DTP software occupies the same space on a line as the daisywheel or NLQ font.

Once you have printed the copy, the text can be cut into columns of the correct length and stuck into position into the blank spaces on the page, using the column rules as a guide to their correct placing.

The result will be an improvement over printing the entire page with a dot–matrix printer. You will have still used your DTP software for the trickiest part of the exercise – designing the page – and you will have achieved a much better quality of print.

8.1 Print enhancers
A print enhancer is software that controls the output of a dot–matrix printer. It does not alter the appearance of the typeface on screen. What you see there is not what you get when you print out the text. The printer's head, as in NLQ printing, makes multiple passes over the paper, building up the character a few dots at a time. This results not only in a greater density of

print, but in a finer control of the shape of the letters. At their best, print enhancers used with a dot-matrix printer will produce print that is virtually indistinguishable from the output of a daisywheel printer.

The advantage over a daisywheel is that different print-styles are obtainable instantly. With a daisywheel, you have to pause the printer, remove the printing wheel and substitute another. Print enhancers normally work by means of embedded commands added to your text.

At their best, print enhancers not only print in a variety of fonts, but in many sizes. Some, too, include font designers so that you can create your own typefaces. They can make great improvements to the quality of text produced with older dot-matrix machines that do not have NLQ printing, and in most cases produce superior results to NLQ output.

A versatile print enhancer provides a useful means of providing headlines for the scissors and paste approach. An alternative is to use transfer lettering which you rubdown into position, letter by letter. But a print enhancer is quicker and easier to use.

An examination of two print enhancers will demonstrate their versatility: one is Permanent Memory Systems' *Multi-Font NTQ* for Acorn's 8-bit BBC and Electron micros; the other is *Lettrix* for the IBM PC and compatibles.

8.1.1 Multi-Font NTQ

Multi-Font NTQ, which describes itself as Near Text Quality Typesetting Software is supplied on two chips which are plugged into the computer's main board, together with a disk containing the font designer. It can be used with any word processor that allows escape sequences (that is, pressing the escape key followed by a letter key) to be sent to an Epson compatible printer. It can also be used from BASIC or other languages that permit control codes to be passed to the printer.

NTQ is supplied with seven different fonts, ranging from a serif typeface and italic to Gothic and Hitech computer. A further eight faces are available. All can be used in 16 different heights and widths, each variable independently. That is, you could have a face 15 times its normal height and five times its normal width so that it was tall and narrow.

The characters can also be underlined and printed at selectable pitches, between 10 and 20 characters to the line, or printed with proportional spacing or micro-justified to provide printing with flush right margins. It is also possible to print the words over 15 different shaded backgrounds, and to print inverse text, white against a black background. Two lines of inverse text can either be printed within a solid block of black or with each line in a separate black box. Its most powerful feature is the macro command, which can be saved to disk, so that complex sequences of control codes can be entered simply, with three key–presses.

NTQ also includes a designer so that users can create their own fonts, with up to eight being worked on simultaneously. Its printed output is excellent, given the limitation that the type looks stepped if enlarged too much, and there is enough variety in its fonts for it to be used with a word processor as a cheap means of desktop publishing. Its drawback is that it is slow to produce results, since the printer makes many passes over the paper. But this objection holds for any dot–matrix printer used with any DTP software.

8.1.2 Lettrix

Lettrix is a memory resident program for the IBM PC and compatibles, so that it is always available when you need it. It lets you design your own fonts and also provides 20 different typefaces which range from Art Deco and those that allow proportional printing, to Greek, Hebrew and Russian alphabets and scientific symbols.

Under the control of *Lettrix*, the dot–matrix printhead makes two passes over the paper. Two key–presses bring up its menu on–screen, from which typefaces and sizes, such as compressed or double–width characters, can be chosen.

You have a choice of selecting from the menu features, such as the spacing between letters, or using commands within your text. *Lettrix* justifies lines by adding spaces between words so that, especially when used with proportional printing, there may be considerable gaps between some words, providing rather too much white space. But the actual quality of its printing comes very close to that of a daisywheel printer.

8.2 Typesetting

The expert way to do–it–yourself is to bypass DTP programs that use interactive pages and go from the computer direct to a typesetter. There are several ways of achieving this, all of which have advantages over conventional methods in which someone sits at a keyboard with your document and keys it in.

When the original has been produced with the aid of a word processor, then the labour of re–keying the manuscript is simply wasted effort. It is time and labour saving to feed the text from the floppy disk on which it is stored into the typesetting machine. Another gain is in accuracy, particularly with a book–length manuscript. Spell–checking and proof–reading programs are available that are compatible with most word processing software so that it is likely that the text will contain few typographical or spelling errors. The most common will be those that only a few proof reading programs will pick up, such as the the the same word printed twice (as "the" was in this sentence).

Inevitably, if someone sits at a keyboard and types in 60,000 or more words, errors will creep in, which will then have to be caught and corrected when the text is in galley proof stage. Murphy's Law – bread always falls buttered side downwards – will ensure as you correct one error, you make another. (A newspaper once carried a correction for printing a story in which a general was described as "battle scared". Of course, the paper said in its apology, what it had meant to write was that the general was "bottle scarred".)

I once had two books going to press at the same time. One, of some 150,000 words, was typeset from my floppy disks. With the other, I delivered a manuscript of 60,000 words, which was set in the conventional manner. The computer–set book contains three typographical errors which I and my spell–checker missed, for some reason. I know why I missed them (sheer carelessness) but I don't understand how my spell–checker overlooked "fela" for "flea".

I hoped my other book contained no errors. But when I checked the proofs I found that more than 40 errors, including lines transposed, had been introduced. The moral is, computer typesetting is best, but don't trust spell checkers because they are dumb.

Preparing a word–processed text for typesetting at its simplest level involves entering embedded commands in the text. The ones I entered were preceded by a backslash, for instance. (Actually, it turned out not to be as simple as I'd hoped, since the word processor I was using also made use of backslashes in command sequences. When it came upon a backslash followed by a sequence it did not understand, it either crashed so that I was left looking at a blank screen or sulked and would not format the text so that I was unable to obtain a print of it. This meant that I had to enter the codes after I had finished writing the text.)

The greatest danger with such a method is entering the codes incorrectly, and remembering to end commands as well as begin them. This also afflicts users of word processors with embedded commands. It is too easy to enter a command to turn on bold or italic text and to forget to turn it off, which means that all subsequent text will print in bold or italic. An alternative is to print the text in the ordinary way, mark how you want it to be printed, in what size or style of type, and leave it to the typesetters to enter the commands. That presupposes that you either understand type or have established precisely what you require from the typesetters.

It is an approach that requires an understanding of typography and is best left to experts. In such cases you cannot see the end result of your labours instantly. You are flying blind. The pleasure provided by programs such as *PageMaker* is that you can see at all times the results of your actions.

8.3 TEX
Another alternative is to use one of the microcomputer versions of Donald Knuth's remarkable *TEX* (pronounced "tech"). Professor Knuth, one of the gurus of computer programming, not only spent eight years writing the language to control complex typesetting, but has also explained it in *Computers and Typesetting* (Addison–Wesley), five volumes of elegant prose.

TEX is a document formatting language which was originally developed to make it easier to typeset mathematical and technical texts which, because of their use of complex equations, can be a nightmare. The program itself, written in Pascal, was placed in the public domain, but you do have to pay for the various microcomputer implementations of it, which run on the IBM PC and compatibles and the Macintosh. You need to create your text on a word processor that allows you to produce ASCII (American Standard Code for Information Interchange) text, which provides a standard numeric means of defining characters.

Into the text you insert commands which will control its typeset appearance. A *TEX* program takes this text and creates the code that will carry out your commands. This code can be fed into a dot–matrix or laser printer or a typesetter, using printer drivers, and will produce identical output, apart from the differences in the quality of the print.

TEX will only run on powerful personal computers. It requires a system with at least 512K of memory and a hard disk. It is a professional typesetting system, and it really requires a professional to run it. A version such as *Textures* for the Macintosh does provide a preview of what will be printed, but you need to appreciate the complexities of typesetting in order to achieve pleasing results. In the hands of expert users, it provides total control over the setting of difficult text.

8.4 Dialtext
The possibilities of computer–controlled typesetting are being enlarged all the time. Many national newspapers are going over to various systems using mainframe computers and others use Macintoshs to create maps and other

art–work to accompany news stories and features. There is at least one British electronic publishing system that is based on a network of Macintosh computers, and which is used to produce the *Poole Advertiser* in Dorset. Talbot Computer's Dialtext system, uses *Newswrite*, software written specifically for use by journalists.

A Macintosh connected to an autodial modem allows copy to be received over the phone from reporters using portable computers, saving money and time in telephone charges.

The software can provide an instant guide to the size of any story that uses the standard settings and the copy can be previewed after editing and before it is sent to a LaserWriter or a phototypesetting machine. Such systems will one day be available to, and affordable by, individuals.

Part Five
Mainly software

Chapter 9: Macintosh & IBM systems

Choosing a desktop publishing system can be difficult. My personal choice, from existing packages I have tried, would be:

- Aldus's *PageMaker* running on the Macintosh.
- Xerox's *Ventura Publisher* running on an IBM XT PC or compatible computer, or IBM's new Model 50 PC.
- Mirrorsoft's *Fleet Street Publisher* running on an Atari 520ST, or a 1040ST or, preferably, on a Mega ST, with a 2Mbyte or a 4Mbyte memory.

In the future the situation may well change. New DTP packages are appearing all the time. It can't be long before the Commodore Amiga has DTP software to match its excellent graphics capabilities; it already has the best art programs of any personal computer.

As with any other software, personal feelings and requirements influence choices. Packages differ from one another not only in such matters as ease of use, but in their capabilities. Some are excellent for producing individual pages that can be put together to form a small newsletter, pamphlet or brochure. Others are more suited for producing book–length documents.

9.1 The ideal desktop publishing program

Ideally, DTP software should combine most of the facilities of a word processor with those of a good graphics program. But both of these requirements are incidental to its main purpose of designing a page or pages and fitting text to it. The laying–out and making up of pages needs to be as close as possible to the physical reality of carrying out such a task. The image on–screen needs to resemble the finished page as it will look when printed.

This WYSIWYG (What You See Is What You Get) approach is both essential and hard to achieve, since the size of a monitor screen does not match that of an A4 sheet of paper. The problem is usually overcome by various degrees of magnification of the finished page. You can get a preview of the whole page in miniature or zoom in to see a part of the actual page exactly as it will appear when printed.

The alternative solution is to buy a special monitor that does resemble, in shape and size, an A4 sheet of white paper. It is useful to be able to see a whole page at a time, since it makes it much easier to spot mistakes. Unfortunately, such monitors cost as much, or even more than, the computers that use them.

There is another answer, which is to use a program where what you see does not resemble what you get. But to operate that requires skill in designing pages away from the screen and is for experts rather than beginners. In a way, it defeats the point of using a microcomputer, which is to allow you to play around with the page design on the screen.

Before considering available programs, it is as well to draw up a check–list of the features an ideal DTP program should have, to provide a standard of comparison.

First, it needs to be compatible with all the standard dot–matrix and laser printers and with *PostScript* so that it can be linked easily to typesetting machines.

Then it requires text–editing facilities. Most DTP programs rely on the words being fed into the program from a word processor. But there needs to be some editing facilities in the program itself to accommodate last minute changes.

These can either be handled on the page, which means that the program must reformat the text after the changes have been made, or by taking the words into a text–editor within the program, making changes and then returning it to the page make–up. In order to be less of a pain, the change from one program to the other should be almost instantaneous.

Virtually all DTP packages allow only black and white printing, partly because until recently the Macintosh, the leading DTP computer, has been a monochrome machine, and partly because high–quality colour printers are extremely expensive. But the option to use colour, although not essential, could be useful.

Like a word processor, the DTP program needs to have, at the very least, the following features:

■ Search and replace – in order to make changes, such as correcting the spelling of a name, throughout the text.
■ Cut and paste – to alter the order of sentences or paragraphs.
■ Delete – to cut text to fit the available space.
■ Copy – to repeat a section of text.

- Headers and footers – to automatically put words at the top or bottom of each page.
- Page numbering – to automatically put numbers on each page.
- Contents creating – automatically producing a table of contents.
- Indexing – to create an index, which can be an extremely useful feature when producing a book. Many word processors allow you to create an index, but transferring it to a DTP program may mean that the page numbers will differ.
- Footnotes – automatically producing footnotes.

In formatting the text on the page, the program needs to allow:
- Text to be centered.
- Text to be set with a ragged right–hand margin.
- Text to be set with a justified right–hand margin.
- Horizontal and vertical justification of text.
- Microjustification, with spaces between letters as well as between words. Preferably, the user should be able to alter the amount of microjustification.
- Adjustable leading between lines.
- Adjustable spacing of individual lines.
- Automatic hyphenation of words, in order to fit them neatly into columns.
- Automatic kerning of letters. If not, it must permit manual kerning.
- Text to flow around graphics on the page.
- Tab settings so that columns of figures can be easily lined up.

There should be a varied collection of type fonts, both for the body of the text and for display use, in headlines. In the use of fonts, it should permit:

- Fonts of any size, within the limits of the page.
- Different size fonts on the same page.
- Different type fonts on the same page.
- Fonts to be set in different styles – bold, italic, outline, reversed, shadow, underlined – and in any mixture of these styles.
- Mathematical signs and symbols.
- Superscript and subscript.

There should be a selection of well–drawn clip art, or ready–made drawings that can be used or altered. These should cover such areas as maps of the world and of continents and countries, people and buildings, arrows and other useful symbols. In the use of graphics, the program should allow:
- Importing graphics created with other programs.
- Graphics of any size.
- Overlaying of text on graphics.
- Cropping and shifting graphics on the page.
- Altering graphics by re–drawing, either on the page or in a graphics editor

that is part of the program and permits quick changes to be made.

There should be decorative features which can be added when wanted:
- Rules of varying sizes between columns.
- Geometric shapes, such as boxes, circles and ellipses.
- Decorative borders.
- Spraying in air–brush style.
- Various shades and patterns which can be used to fill boxes as a background to text or graphics.

Lastly, come the features that make page design easy:
- Multiple units of measurements – in inches, millimetres, picas, points.
- Templates that can be set up for a succession of pages, covering the size of the paper, the size of margins, the size and number of columns on the page.
- A grid that can be toggled on or off, to aid in the placement of text and graphics.
- A "snap to" feature so that columns or graphics move automatically to the nearest grid line.
- A link feature, so that text will flow automatically from one column or page to the next.
- A preview facility, so that you can see precisely what the finished page will look like. Ideally, you should be able to preview more than one page at a time, since good design requires the left–hand and right–hand pages to be considered together.
- The ability to move text and graphics off the page but keep them in view so that quick re–designs of pages can be made.
- An indication that all the text fits into the space allocated, or whether there is some left over.
- The ability to delete text or graphics from the page.

There is no program that has all these facilities, but the list is useful beginning when you are shopping around for a DTP program. It provides a standard for comparison.

Ideally, you should be able to load into a DTP program text or graphics from virtually any source – with most you cannot. The exceptions are the Macintosh and the Commodore Amiga, where standard means of storing files, particularly graphics, have been established from the start. At the moment the Amiga's DTP software does not match the best available for the Macintosh. When it does, the Amiga could be a formidable rival.

Computing can be seen not so much as involving rivalry between manufacturers, although of course it does, as between microprocessors. In 8–bit machines, the battle was between the 6502 processor – as found in the

Apple II, Atari XE, Acorn's BBC machines and the Commodore 64 – and the Z80, which powers the Sinclair Spectrums, the Amstrad CPCs and PCWs, and all those many makes of business micro running the CP/M operating system and software.

In 16– and 32–bit computing, the struggle for supremacy is between Motorola's 68000 series – to be found in the Apple Macintosh, the Commodore Amiga and the Atari ST – and Intel's 8088 processor and its successors, which was what IBM chose for its PCs and is found in the many compatible computers such as the Amstrad PC 1512.

Of the two, the 68000 seems to me to have produced far more exciting computers, ones that are easier and more pleasurable to use. They score in desktop publishing because the 68000 computers are graphics orientated. They use visual devices to make it easier for users to control them – the pictorial approach known as WIMPs, standing for Windows, Icons, Mouse, Pull down menus.

The mouse, a small rectangular object with buttons on the top and a ball underneath, is at the heart of the system. By moving it along the desk you control the movement of a pointer on the screen. By pointing at an icon (a small symbol that can represent a program or an action such as deleting a file), and clicking on one of the mouse buttons, you can load a program or carry out the action. You can also use the mouse to pull down an on–screen menu, or list, of actions which can be carried out by pointing and clicking on the mouse.

Windows are sections of the screen which can be used to display the output from different programs or from different aspects of one program.

Apple brought this environment into popular use with its Macintosh computer. IBM has belatedly caught up with it, so that its latest machines, launched in April 1987, all have a mouse as standard equipment and will have windows and the rest of the WIMP environment when the computer's new operating system is finished. Many IBM compatible computers, such as the Amstrad PC, use a similar operating system, Digital Research's *GEM* (for Graphics Environment Manager).

The Macintosh, unlike most computers before it, treats text and graphics in the same way. It is a bit–mapped system. To get decent graphics from an IBM PC you need to add various graphics boards and costly enhancements.

As a result, whereas you know the Macintosh will work with all DTP software written for the machine, with an IBM PC you need to check that a particular program will work with your configuration. The graphics standard on the newest IBM computers is a great improvement. But, I feel, the 68000 machines are likely to remain easier to use. Nevertheless, IBM is determined to become a force in desktop publishing and will no doubt do so, thanks to its commercial muscle and the many people who already use IBM PCs and compatible computers.

9.2 Apple's Macintosh

The Macintosh has gone through many changes since it was first launched in 1984, although in certain respects it remains unchanged. You can view the alterations as evolutionary, a natural progression, or as Apple's continuing attempts to get right a machine that was conceptually correct but electronically flawed.

The first Macintosh was underpowered. Its 128K memory was too small; in use, it was sluggish. Later models can still be slow, particularly in some of the more memory demanding complexities of desktop publishing.

What was unique about the machine was its WIMP interface, its small size which made it easy to carry around (the disk drive and processor were all contained in the monitor case). It had a monochrome display, so that the screen, with its black text on a white background, resembled a sheet of paper.

Its disadvantage was that it was a closed system, with but one disk drive. Virtually nothing could be added to the machine because it lacked expansion slots. Its small size also meant that it had a 9 inch display, which can seem very tiny indeed. The first Macintosh was superseded first by the Fat Mac, which had 512K memory and then the Macintosh Plus, a machine with 1Mbyte of memory, two disk drives and facilities that allowed hard disks to be connected easily.

In April, 1987 Apple produced its latest models: the Macintosh SE (for System Enhanced) and the Macintosh II, a more powerful computer using the 68020 microprocessor and with six expansion slots, which can accommodate a co–processor so that it will run software written for the IBM PC. The Macintosh SE looks much like its predecessors, except that it has twin disk drives, one above the other. There is room for an internal 20Mbyte hard disk. It has 1Mbyte of memory, which can be expanded to 4Mbytes and Apple claims that it is faster than previous models.

The Macintosh II is a much heftier machine, not easily portable. It is the first Mac to have colour and comes with a 12 inch monochrome or a 13 inch colour monitor. It can have two disk drives as well as a hard disk of up to 80Mbyte and is capable of addressing memory of up to 4 Gigabytes. That is as powerful as most people will ever want. For desktop publishing, a Mac with a minimum of 512K memory is needed. Some software will also require a second disk drive. A hard disk is useful, but not essential.

9.2.1 Macintosh DTP software

Apple created the business of desktop publishing with the Macintosh. The machine was originally sold with a word processor, *MacWrite*, which was in many ways limited, but did allow different styles of type to be used. It hinted at new possibilities.

These were realised in the program that has become the standard for desktop publishing, Aldus's *PageMaker*. IBM has recently endorsed *PageMaker*, in its IBM version, as the program it will be selling as part of a DTP package. *PageMaker*, then, can be considered the tops. It certainly was the best program. Whether it still is, is another matter. Rival companies have taken note of the best features of *PageMaker* and incorporated them in their own programs, improving on them as they did so. DTP packages are now appearing at an astounding rate, each trying to outdo the other.

At the same time, word processing packages are beginning to incorporate many of the features of desktop publishing, so that the distinction between the two kinds of programs is beginning to blur. Depending upon your needs, one of the latest word processors might meet your requirements. If not, then PageMaker is the program you should probably investigate first.

How does it measure up to the ideal? Quite well. But that is not surprising since, more than any other program, it defined what features a DTP package should have . It falls down on its text editing It does not include a sophisticated, or even an unsophisticated, text editor. The words need to be written with a word processor, such as *MacWrite* or Microsoft's *Word*, and then loaded into the program. Within *PageMaker* you can add a few words or delete what is there, but no more than that.

Nor can you touch up drawings or illustrations from within the program. You need an art program such as *MacPaint* or *MacDraw* to produce graphics. *PageMaker* does have a few built-in drawing features, but these are to add boxes or borders. You can draw lines, boxes (with square or rounded corners), circles or ellipses and fill them with patterns or textures in shades of grey.

PageMaker is compatible with *PostScript*. It can handle paper in A4 size, American Letter (8.5 x 11 inches or 21.6 x 27.9 cm), American Legal (8.5 x 14 inches or 21.6 x 35.6 cm), or Tabloid (11 x 16.75 inches or 27.9 x 42.5 cm). The screen display shows a page in miniature, a toolbox on the right –

providing a menu of various operations such as placing column guides – and space on the left, corresponding to an actual desktop to hold text.

The page can be viewed in its entirety on screen, for an overview how the layout will look. In order to check on the precise placement of text and graphics it can be seen on various levels of magnification. At these levels, of course, you can see only part of a page at a time, but you can edit what you see.

Before the text can be loaded on to the page, you need to specify the number of columns of text and guides – vertical lines marking the edge of the columns – required. Text or graphics are loaded from a floppy or hard disk and placed on the page by clicking on the mouse button and dragging them into position.

A plus mark at the end of column of text on the page indicates that the text is longer than the specified space. By clicking on the text column, the text will flow into it. Text can be easily moved within the columns.

You can specify what text or graphics, such as titles or headings, are to appear on every page. The pages can be automatically numbered, and the program can handle up to 128 pages at a time. A grid to which lines or text snap can be added to each page. A spread of a left– and right–hand page can be previewed. The units of measurement used are inches, millimetres, picas and points.

Type can be used in all styles, including superscript and subscript. The Macintosh has a good selection of built–in fonts, which can be used in virtually any size. If you're using *PageMaker* with a laser printer then your choice will be limited to the printer's, rather than the computer's fonts.

Aldus has recently issued version 2.0 of its program, which now has automatic hyphenation and kerning. In all, *PageMaker* is a comprehensive program that meets most requirements. It does require the backup of a word processor and a graphics program.

Ready Set Go was one of *PageMaker's* earliest rivals. It was the poorer program. But it has since been extensively rewritten and in its latest version – 3.0 – is good enough for Letraset, which had already chosen another program to endorse, to drop its first choice and take it over.

In its latest form it can match *PageMaker* in many respects and has the advantage of being much cheaper. Like *PageMaker*, it contains little in the way of graphics facilities, other than the ability to draw lines, rectangles, circles and ellipses. Drawings need to be prepared in a program such as *MacDraw* and they can be re-sized or cropped on the page.

It does have a full word processor, including a spelling checker, so that text can be entered directly into a page. Words can also be imported from *MacWrite* or *Word*. It provides a similar display to *PageMaker*, showing a blank page and a toolkit, this time down the lefthand side of the screen, enabling you to carry out such functions as inserting text, drawing rectangles or indicating that the text should flow from one column to another. As in *PageMaker*, the page can be viewed at different magnifications. You can define a master page with specific features, such as headings or footings and pages can be numbered automatically.

Measurements are provided in inches, centimetres and picas. A series of boxes allows you to specify details of the layout, such as size of margins or width of columns without having to draw them. A layout grid with a snap to feature for aligning columns or graphics is available.

Text can be made to flow around any shape on the page, so that if you add an illustration then the text automatically reforms itself around it. It allows automatic or manual kerning, automatic hyphenation, and is *PostScript* compatible. In all, *RSG-3* is an excellent program, a great advance on its predecessors, both powerful and easy to use.

Mindscape's *ComicWorks* is probably the most fun of all DTP packages, at least for those who enjoy Superman or Judge Dredd-style comics. *GraphicWorks* applies the same techniques to the duller but worthy field of business presentation.

ComicWorks is a design program for producing comic books, although it can be used for producing anything that mixes text and graphics. As with a comic, each page contains panels which can hold either text, in areas called balloons, or graphics, in areas known as easels.

A panel, which can be of any shape and bigger than a page in size, can hold up to 64 easels and balloons. Balloons come in 18 different shapes, six of which can also be customised. Included is a good selection of clip art, created by Mike Saenz, in classic comic book style, with intrepid, flash spacemen, voluptuous female helpers and threatening bug-eyed monsters. There are also several comic book fonts to provide the appropriate kind of lettering.

These drawings can be arranged or altered to fit an invented story. The program includes a good art program, similar in some respects to *MacPaint*, to spray dots in airbrush styles, add patterns, draw lines of various thickness, or outlined and filled rectangles, ovals and polygons.

Drawings can be cut, copied and pasted, inverted or rotated and rescaled to smaller or larger sizes. Layouts can be saved as templates for further use. Panels can be re-sized or dragged around the page. Within the panels, graphics and text can be overlaid to build up complex pictures and speech bubbles.

The pages can be previewed two at a time, although it is not possible to edit them in this mode. The program also includes programs to print a page in greetings card format or as a poster, when the page can be enlarged by 3200 per cent or reduced to one per cent of its original size.

There is a grid with a snap to feature for aligning your work and measurement is in inches, centimetres or pixels. *ComicWorks* is compatible with graphics created with *MacPaint* and the results can be printed with an ImageWriter or LaserWriter.

GraphicWorks is an identical program, except that it is supplied with more sober predefined templates which can be used for creating newsletters, restaurant menus, advertisements, forms, labels and invoices.

Ragtime is a more specialised DTP package that includes its own spreadsheet, which makes it useful for those whose work includes the presentation of tabulated information.

9.2.2 Macintosh document processing software

In response to the challenge of desktop publishing systems, word processing software is becoming more complex, allowing the integration of text and graphics and the setting of words into multiple columns.

Microsoft's *Word 3.0* for the Macintosh is probably the most powerful word processor available for personal computers. It allows the user to define the sizes of pages and margins and to create various styles for paragraphs, covering such aspects as fonts and line lengths.

Graphics can be imported from other programs and re-sized. *Word* can set words in multiple columns, provide previews of what a double-page spread will look like when printed and will create contents tables and indexes.

It is capable of setting complex formulae and equations and has virtually every feature anyone could want, apart from the astounding omission of a word count. *Word 3.0* is *PostScript* compatible and could well meet many users' desktop publishing needs. Its only rival is the much cheaper *MacAuthor*, which also allows the user to set and store styles for paragraphs and headings.

9.3 IBM PC and compatibles

In the beginning, IBM seems to have aimed its PC at home users, which no doubt accounted for its shortcomings: the first PCs could only address 640K of memory directly. They were austere machines in many ways, lacking the graphics and sound facilities found on many computers. The IBM PC was an open system. It needed to be, with companies making expansion boards to provide colour in addition to the monochrome display, and to improve the quality of the graphics.

All the add-ons have made IBM an expensive buy for individuals, although the existence of cheaper, or better, compatible computers, or clones, has reinforced its position as the standard business micro.

It has taken until 1987 for IBM to produce computers with a good graphics resolution built in. The Personal System/2 series – Models 30, 50, 60 and 80 – offer the sort of performance that makes them suitable for desktop publishing. The Model 30 resembles the older-style PC/XT and has a resolution of up to 640 x 480 in monochrome and 320 x 200 in 256 colours. The Model 50, which has 1Mbyte of RAM, has the same monochrome resolution and an improved colour one – 640 x 480 in 256 colours.

The latest IBM hardware is in advance of software. The new PC/2 machines can theoretically support multi-tasking so that you can have more than one program running at the same time. MS-DOS OS/2, the new operating system that will permit this, however, is not expected to be available until 1988.
For desktop publishing purposes, the minimum requirements are an IBM PC/AT or compatible with 512K memory, an EGA or similar graphics card, and a hard disk.

9.3.1 IBM DTP software

Xerox's *Ventura Publisher*, which runs under Digital Research's *GEM* interface is an excellent package for speedily producing long documents, such as books or brochures. *GEM* gives it something of the feel of Macintosh software. But its ease of use in such situations comes from a different emphasis than that of other DTP packages.

Ventura uses style sheets, which are files defining the details of page layouts. Accompanying the system are 21 different style sheets for producing such publications as reports, brochures, newsletters and technical documents. The style sheets define the layout in general terms. But within the style sheets are additional formats, known as tags, which cover the style to be used for specifics, such as headlines and captions.

These sheets can be applied to a complete document, so that as the text is loaded in, it is fitted into the chosen style, flowing from one page to the next.

You can then tag sections of the text that are to serve as byline or headlines or cross heads and they will be reformatted in the chosen style. Text can either be transferred from word processors, including *WordPerfect, Word, Multimate* and *WordStar*, or typed in on the page. *Ventura* allows basic word processing for moving text, or deleting and inserting it.

Measurement is in inches, centimetres, picas and points. Graphics need to be created with such programs as *GEM Draw, Gem Paint, PC Paintbrush* and *Autocad. Ventura* itself has a few limited graphics functions, mainly to add lines, boxes and circles or to put tints behind the text.

Graphics are loaded into frames, which are boxes that you draw on the page, or define by entering its size. Surrounding text is re-formatted to flow around the boxes. Frames can hold text as well as graphics.

All information concerning the style and tag sheets and the text files is stored in a chapter file, and the chapters can be grouped to make a publication, which can be up to 64 chapters long. *Ventura* will add numbers for pages, figures and chapters and will create a contents table and index. Its screen display shows you two pages at a time in miniature or part of one page.

Thanks to its style sheets, *Ventura* lets you feed in a long text file and create a professional-looking document with greater ease than any other package. With its predefined formats, it is probably the easiest package to use for those uncertain of their design skills. It is compatible with *PostScript* and also Xerox's *Interpress* page description language.

Aldus's *PageMaker* is available for the IBM PC in its version 2, which has the same features as the Macintosh program. Mindscape's two Macintosh programs *ComicWorks* and *GraphicWorks* will be available in IBM versions soon. (For more details, see Macintosh DTP software above.)

Harvard Professional Publisher – too new for me to have tried – is, like *Ventura*, designed for the production of long documents. Its specifications include automatic hyphenation and kerning, adjustable leading, control of widows and orphans, automatic page numbering, the flowing of text through pages or an entire document and vertical justification. It also allows multiple columns, variable rules and boxes and the creation of style sheets. It is *PostScript* compatible.

Digital Research has announced *GEM Desktop Publisher*, a program which incorporates the *First Word Plus* word processing software. The features it offers appear, from the specifications, to provide no more than Mirrorsoft's *Fleet Street Editor*, which is the most versatile low–cost DTP software for the IBM PC so far available. *Desktop Publisher* is, however, compatible with *Ventura Publisher* and could be used with it as part of a multi–user set–up.

The cheapest program is *Fontasy*, which is closer in its approach to the exuberance of Victorian jobbing printers than cool professionalism of *Ventura Publisher*. Its display fonts, starred and striped like the American flag, or which can be framed in Christmas decorations, are not for serious use, although you can create your own with the font editor included in its toolkit disk.

You can add text and draw simple graphics within the program, create templates to be used as the basis for page design and import text from other word processors providing it is in ASCII format. It is a splendid tool for the creation of posters or handbills.

9.3.2 IBM PC document processing software
Lotus's *Manuscript* is a document processor designed for the production of long technical and business reports and manuals. It lacks some of the qualities of desktop publishing, for you cannot set words in multiple columns, although you can put numerical information into tables.

But it does include some unusual and extremely useful features, notably its Document Compare which, as its name suggests, compares two versions of the same document and highlights the differences between them.

You can include graphics within the document, set mathematical equations and easily reformat an entire document – changing the type size of all headings, for instance – or sections of it. You can preview pages and print the result on dot–matrix or laser printers. *Manuscript*, which requires a hard disk, is *PostScript* compatible.

Running under *GEM*, *1st Word Plus* is a good, inexpensive word processor that allows the integration of text and graphics and may suffice for those wishing to produce short, uncomplicated documents containing simple illustrations.

Chapter 10: Cheaper systems

For those who cannot afford either a Macintosh or an IBM or compatible fitted with the necessary extras to make it capable of coping with the demands of the best quality desktop publishing, there are many cheaper alternatives.

Potentially, at least, the Atari ST and the Commodore Amiga, both using the same Motorola 68000 chip as the Macintosh, are capable of equalling the printed output of any personal computer. Both are superior in graphics handling to the IBM PC. Both are much cheaper. Both have available for them good software that is also much cheaper than the IBM's or the Mac's and can drive laser printers.

The savings in cost can be considerable. You can buy an 512K Atari ST, a dot–matrix printer and good DTP software for around the same price as *Ventura Publisher* costs for an IBM PC. An Amiga 500 is cheaper than *Harvard Professional Publisher* DTP software for the IBM.

The Atari Mega ST will be able to drive Atari's low–cost laser printer, which will require the Mega's large memory capacity to control it. Commodore has hinted that it may produce its own laser printer in the near future, but equally it may not, since its frequent management changes affect its future plans. Available Amiga DTP software is compatible with *PostScript* so that it will work with many laser printers.

Among the less powerful 8–bit computers, Britain's favourite word–processing computer the Amstrad PCW has a good DTP program, as has the Amstrad CPC. Acorn's BBC micro was the first computer after the Macintosh to have DTP programs written for it.

So far, no one seems to have produced good DTP programs for the Apple, presumably because of the dominance of the Macintosh, and I have not been impressed by programs available for the Commodore 64. DTP software for the Commodore is improving, though. Rarely has serious software penetrated all levels of personal computing so swiftly.

For many 8–bit computers are to be found different versions of two programs, Advanced Memory Systems' *Stop Press* and Mirrorsoft's *Fleet*

Street Editor. Both are excellent programs, given the limitations of the machines on which they run, with *Fleet Street Editor* notable for the high quality of its accompanying manuals, which explain the program's workings clearly and concisely.

10.1 Atari ST DTP software

After some unsatisfactory early models, the Atari ST has emerged as the least expensive 16–bit computer providing considerable power and more than adequate memory. The Atari ST has much the same processing power as the Macintosh. It substitutes Digital Research's similar *GEM* for the Mac's WIMP environment. It feels like a less sophisticated computer, although the Mega STs may change that, and much of its software lacks the refinement and brilliance of the Macintosh.

There is no reason why, in the long term, it should not be able to compete with a standard Macintosh, particularly as it provides colour, although none of the available DTP software makes use of this facility.

The Atari ST comes in versions with a 512K memory, as in the 520 model, or a 1024K memory, as in the 1040 ST. Either, preferably used with a monochrome monitor, is sufficient for desktop publishing. Better, though, are the two Mega STs which are in three parts: keyboard, a unit containing the microprocessor and disk drive, and monitor.

The Mega STs have either 2Mbyte or 4Mbyte memories and, because they can also control the Atari laser printer, are the obvious choice for desktop publishing. It is possible to use the ordinary STs and link them to laser printers. It may even turn out to be preferable, but no one will know for sure until the Atari printer is available and working.

There is a choice of two DTP packages: Mirrorsoft's *Fleet Street Publisher* and SoftLogik's *Publishing Partner*. Available for both are drivers for *PostScript*-compatible laser printers. Both DTP packages are good. *Publishing Partner* has superior drivers for dot–matrix printers which smooth some of the more jagged edges from the bit–mapped characters before printing them.

Fleet Street Publisher provides a greater degree of control over the placing and justification of text, and for that reason, and the fact it is cheaper, is the best package available so far for the ST. The program supports automatic hyphenation and kerning, but to use these facilities you will need an ST with a hard disk. The criteria for hyphenation can be set by the user. The program works on one page at a time and will not carry text over to succeeding pages. You can define the size of a page, set the margins and the number and width of the columns and the size of the gutter. You can also adjust the leading above and below a line of type and condense and expand any particular typeface. There are 12 typefaces supplied, in sizes that range from 4 to 72 point.

Text can be loaded from other word processors or typed into a text editor which has some word processing functions. In order to lay out a page you define blocks, which can contain either text or graphics. Blocks can be re-sized or moved around the page.

Changing the size or position of the blocks can also be done once the words and pictures are in position. Frames and rules can be added to the blocks. The program has no graphics facilities, other than the ability to draw or erase at single pixel level. But pictures can be rotated as well as re-sized.

Clip art, ranging from maps and weather symbols to pouting girls and screaming jets, is provided. The program contains a driver for Epson-compatible 9 pin dot-matrix printers. A *PostScript*-compatible driver for laser printers is also available. *Fleet Street Publisher 2*, an enhanced version described as "a fully professional desktop publishing system", is scheduled for release during 1987.

Publishing Partner allows you to type text onto the page, or it can be loaded from a word processor that uses ASCII format. Text can flow across columns and pages if required. There is no automatic hyphenation, but soft hyphenation is supported and you can adjust kerning and leading. Pages can be viewed at various levels of magnification.

Graphics are best created in an art program, since its drawing facilities are limited, but the imported images can be re-sized. A selection of adequate clip art is included. It is possible to obtain a colour print with *Publishing Partner*, if it is linked to a suitable printer. Drivers for *PostScript*-compatible and other laser printers are supplied with the program. The quality of its dot-matrix print is better than in any comparable package, particularly with its drivers for the NEC range of 24 pin printers, which reach a resolution of 360 dpi.

10.1.2 Atari ST document processing software

Signum, which is the most expensive text editing program for the ST, is a WYSIWYG document processor producing a very high quality of printed output from dot-matrix printers, and which can be linked to laser printers by the additional purchase of a printer driver. When used with the NEC Pinwriter range of dot-matrix machines, with their 24-pin printheads, its print resolution is 360 dpi, which is higher than the resolution provided by a laser printer. Because *Signum* utilises a dot–matrix printer's graphic mode, the printing speed is slow, although bearable. *Signum* provides some attractive fonts, with a maximum of seven allowed in any one document, and can print Greek, mathematical and graphic symbols.

The program includes a font editor, and any font can be italicised, enlarged, reduced and made bold. Its control over the placing of text is excellent, with small increments allowed in horizontal and vertical movement and in word and character spacing. Graphics of a kind are possible, since large characters can be built up from smaller ones to create circles, squares and similar shapes. But it does not provide the integration of text and graphics that a DTP package does.

For the production of documents consisting largely of text arranged in pages, it produces excellent results. It requires an Atari ST with 1Mbyte of memory and a monochrome monitor and any dot–matrix printer which is completely compatible with the Epson printers.

A cheaper but versatile document processor (seen in an uncompleted version) is *Calligrapher*, which allows the integration of text and graphics, multi-column setting of text and the use of different type styles and sizes. *GEM*-based, *Calligrapher* can use any *GEM* fonts and drive any *GEM* output device, which will include Atari's laser printer. It also shows on screen what you get when you print out the document. Graphics can be scaled on the page and boxes and borders put around text.

It includes all the usual facilities of word processing software, together with a graphics–orientated outline planner for organising the structure of a document or article. Automatic hyphenation is provided, if wanted, and text can be justified or centered. Computer Concepts, the publisher of *Calligrapher*, plans to provide laser printing and scanning services to users of the program.

Also *GEM*-based is SoftTechnics' *DeskWrite*, an accessory program that can reside in memory at the same time as other programs and be called up when needed. It allows the integration of text and graphics and the use of up to four different fonts in any document. The *GEM*-based *1st Word Plus* word processing program can set text in multi–columns, has a WYSIWYG screen display and can incorporate graphics so that it can be used for producing illustrated pamphlets of an uncomplicated kind.

10.3 Commodore Amiga DTP software
The Amiga, as with other new computers, has gone through several changes since it first appeared. The original machine, the Amiga 1000, is likely to be

dropped, giving way to two newer machines. All Amigas use a mouse and have their own WIMP environment, known as Intuition, which allows multiple windows to be opened and moved around on-screen.

The Amiga 500 is aimed at the home user. The bigger Amiga 2000 is intended for business use. The A500 resembles the Commodore 128 in appearance. It comes with 512K of memory, which can easily be expanded to 1Mbyte, and has a disk drive built into the keyboard.

The Amiga 2000 offers internal expansion, which was not possible with the A1000, which requiring users to add peripherals rather than plug boards inside. It has 1Mbyte of memory, a separate keyboard and a main unit that can take a mixture of 3.5 inch and 5.25 inch disk drives as well as hard disks. The most unusual feature is that, with the addition of a special board, it is compatible with the IBM PC. Because the Amiga is a multi-tasking computer, it is possible to have IBM and Amiga programs running simultaneously.

Many of the qualities that make the Amiga an outstanding computer, such as its sound chip, its speech synthesis, its superb graphics capabilities, are irrelevant for the purposes of desktop publishing. It is nevertheless a powerful computer, using the same 68000 processor as the Macintosh and Atari ST and, thanks to its custom chips, outperforming them in most respects. What it lacks is software. There are brilliant graphics programs available for it, and some excellent sound ones. But there is no solid body of serious software, although much is promised.

At the Amiga's launch in 1986, several desktop publishing systems were mentioned as being in preparation. Most of them have turned out to belong to that category known as vapourware, programs which are announced, but which never actually appear.

DTP software for the Amiga will run on a machine with a 512K memory and a single disk drive. Because of the way its operating system works, it is a frustrating machine to use with a single drive. For peace of mind, you need a machine with two disk drives or an expanded memory so that a RAM disk can be set up to hold the operating system commands.

There is but one DTP program, *PageSetter*, currently available, with another two, *Publisher 1000* and *City Desk*, on the point of release. *PageSetter* offers users a similar interface as programs such as *PageMaker* or *RSG-3*, except that it is more promising than perfected.

The display screen shows a blank page with space at one side to hold surplus text or graphics and a row of icons which allow different actions to be carried out. The layout can be measured in picas or inches, and the page can be displayed at different degrees of magnification, with editing changes possible at all levels. It uses a system of boxes, which are similar to the Amiga's windows in that they can be of any size and moved around the screen, to hold either text or graphics.

To use a box, you simply draw it on the page at whatever size you require. When its size, which can be as big as a page, is changed the text within it is re-formatted. By clicking on boxes with the mouse, text can flow from one column or page to another.

Boxes can be placed one on top of the other and made opaque or transparent so that text can be easily overlaid on graphics. There is an alternative method of defining the layout of a page by entering the number of columns required and their size. You can define a default page in this way, which will automatically be set up when you create a new page. The style of boxes can be defined in a similar way.

PageSetter includes a separate text editor, with most of the features of a word processor, in which you can either create or load your text from other word processors. It is a line–oriented program, which means that an efficient typist will be able to enter text faster than it can be displayed on screen. By the use of embedded commands within the text editor you can have the type set in different styles, such as bold, italic, shadowed or outline.

Movement between the text editor and the page layout is almost instantaneous and text is shifted from one to the other as quickly. If you need to make changes to the text, it has to be returned to the editor first. Graphics are handled in the same way, through a graphics editor which includes all the standard tools of drawing. Text as well as images can be manipulated by the editor. A selection of clip art is included.

Because graphics are stored on the Amiga in a standard format, illustrations can be imported from any other graphics program. The editor converts colour graphics to monochrome ones by substituting various tints for the colours so that the results are unpredictable.

Handling of graphics is the weakest point of *PageSetter*, since a full–screen picture in the editor translates into something less than a quarter of a page when moved from the editor to the page layout. It is possible to move the graphic, to frame it and to crop it. But it cannot be made larger.

Other failings are the lack of automatic hyphenation and kerning. Soft hyphenation is possible, as is manual kerning. Leading and letter–spacing can be adjusted with ease. Other early weaknesses, such as its total reliance on the Amiga's system fonts, are being rectified. *PageSetter* is an easy program to use, which is just as well, since its manual is appalling.

If its handling of graphics is improved and automatic hyphenation and kerning is provided, then it should be usable at a professional level. *PageSetter LaserScript*, a *PostScript*–compatible printer driver, is available as a separate program. It includes a utility to reduce the size of pages and to overlay them on other pages to create unusual effects.

Gold Disk, the publisher of *PageSetter*, has announced a more advanced program Professional Page that will be able to display all of the Amiga's 4096 colours, as well as providing automatic hyphenation and kerning. The company is also working on a colour module for the program that will be able to handle colour correction and to produce four colour separated sheets ready for plates and printing.

Publisher 1000, which is being sold under the aggressive slogan "Move Over Mac", is not yet available in Britain. It will allow users to draw graphics directly on a page and to set type in multi–columns over multiple pages. A *PostScript*–compatible printer driver for the program will be forthcoming. Also announced is *City Desk*, which, according to its specification, will offer all the facilities you might expect from a DTP package, including kerning and *PostScript* compatibility.

Viewed in a beta–test version, *City Desk* had better graphics handling than *PageSetter* and made use of embedded codes to handle changes in type–styles and fonts, which should provide for greater precision in type–setting. The newest program is *Shakespeare*, which allows the use of colour, includes graphic design templates to aid page layout, and can drive *PostScript*–compatible laser printers.

10.2.1 Amiga document processing software

Vizawrite (seen in various incomplete version for the past year) will permit the integration of text and graphics and the use of different fonts, as well as the more usual functions of word processing software. It is intended as the nucleus of a complete desktop publishing system that Viza is developing for the Amiga.

ProWrite is one of the few word processors which is designed for colour printing. It also allows for text and graphics to be integrated and shows on screen the document exactly as it will be printed. A disadvantage is that it uses the Amiga's high resolution display, which can cause an annoying flicker unless used with a special monitor. A new version of the program, which can be used at medium resolution and so avoid the screen flicker, has been released, but it is no longer fully WYSIWYG.

10.3 Amstrad CPC

For desktop publishing, you really need to use the CPC6128 as other models do not have a big enough memory. AMS's *Stop Press* is the only DTP package so far available, although a version of *Fleet Street Editor* will be released during 1987.

Stop Press requires a CPC6128 or a 464 and 664 with a 64K memory expansion (and a disk drive for the 464). It can be controlled from the keyboard or by a joystick or mouse. Text can be entered from the keyboard or loaded from word processors. One advanced feature is that text can be made to fill any enclosed shape, including circles and triangles.

There is a character designer, which doubles as a font editor, to add to a comprehensive selection of 22 supplied, although only three can be accessed at any one time. A graphics editor contains standard drawing tools as well as the ability to manipulate images. There is a magnification feature for modifying graphics at the level of single pixels.

Layout is done on a full page, by defining columns and boxes to hold text or graphics. Only a part of the page can be seen at any one time. A preview function lets you view a complete page.

The program includes a varied selection of clip art and is compatible with a video digitiser so that digitised images can be loaded into the graphics editor for manipulation.

10.4 Amstrad PCW

The Amstrad PCW is sold as a word processing computer complete with printer so that desktop publishing seems a natural extension of its possibilities. A disadvantage is that it is difficult to use the machine with any other printer. The quality of print from a PCW's printer is of a reasonable standard, but cannot match the output of 24–pin printers.

The best DTP package so far available is *Fleet Street Editor Plus*. The cheapest, and excellent value, is Database's *The Desktop Publisher*, which includes a text and graphics editor. A version of *Stop Press*, already available for the Amstrad CPC computers, will be released in the near future. *FSE Plus* will work with the PCW's printer or with any Epson-compatible printer with a Centronics interface, or laser printers in dot-matrix mode. It includes a text editor and a graphics editor where you can prepare words and pictures for your page. Files from the PCW's resident word processing program *Locoscript* can be imported.

Up to seven columns can be put on a page and up to five fonts in different styles can be used. Within the text editor, you define the column width you want and the text is then entered formatted to that width. A measure of the depth of the column is provided so that you can edit the words to the required length.

The graphics editor allows you to manipulate images and text, and a good selection of clip art is included. Once illustrations have been chosen, they have to be copied to another disk for inclusion in the page layout.

Page layouts are done by defining the limits of the page, which sets the boundaries of text or graphics blocks. These blocks can be of any size, although text contained within them must be of the same font and size, so that separate blocks are required for headings and the body text.

If your publication is intended to be printed with double-sided pages, the program adjusts the margins to provide wider spacing on the gutter to allow for binding or stapling.

A page style, with blocks allocated for text and graphics, can be defined, but only one style is allowed for any one publication. You see on the screen part of the page at any one time, but you cannot preview a complete page in its entirety . The program can handle soft hyphenation and manual kerning. Justification and leading is done automatically.

10.5 BBC B/Compact/Master

Acorn's BBC computer has established itself as the leading educational computer in Britain. The now discontinued BBC B, which remains the dominant machine, had a 32K memory. It was replaced by 64K and 128K versions and then the Master, which has 128K, and the Compact, a 3.5 inch disk-based, cut-down version of the Master.

Available DTP software was written for the 32K machine and has not been changed to take advantage of the bigger memories of the later models. There are two dominant programs: the ubiquitous *Fleet Street Editor* and *Stop Press* (which was originally called *Pagemaker*).

It is difficult to recommend one over the other, since both have different strengths and weaknesses. *FSE* is supplied on two disks; *Stop Press* comes on two disks and two ROMs which plug into the computer's main board so that you will require spare ROM sockets in order to use it. *FSE* takes a slightly more cumbersome approach by dividing the publishing process into several distinct steps: preparing text, preparing graphics, merging the two. As a result, there is a great deal of loading and reloading, of moving words and pictures from one part of the program to another.

The approach to layout is idiosyncratic. Its greatest disadvantage is that it limits page design to one or two columns. A page is divided into six separate blocks. Each block of text and graphics can be placed across one or two columns, a two column approach then giving three blocks to a page.

The layout within a block can be flexible. The restraints on design do have some advantages. As each block is a separate entity, blocks can be saved individually to disk and used to form the basis of other pages. It makes it possible to store easily title blocks for regular features in publications.

FSE is supplied with a good selection of fonts and clip art, and further fonts and graphics have been published. Its strength lies in the control it provides over the arrangement of text, which is superior to that of *Stop Press*.

Stop Press provides a scrolling screen, showing the page at full size on which text and graphics are placed, which gives a far greater flexibility of layout. One great advantage is that you can have as many columns as you like on a page. Layout is simply a matter of drawing boxes on the page and putting text or graphics in them. The price you pay is in the rigidity with which the program stores completed page. It is far harder to set up templates to be used in a regular publication. The justification of text is crude, so that it is easy to leave rivers of white space running through the page.

10.6 Commodore 64/128
The most venerable, as well as the most popular, of home computers the Commodore 64 has the disadvantage of a tortoise–slow disk drive when used for any serious computing purposes. This restriction also applies to the compatible Commodore 128 when used in its Commodore 64. The more versatile 128 is three computers in one: a Commodore 64; a Commodore 128, although there is not much software available for it on its own account; and a CP/M machine. Again, very little CP/M software has been transferred to the 128's format.

Until recently the only DTP package available for the C64 was *Newsroom*, a package that allows text and graphics to be mixed on the page. But it is not easy to produce very attractive results. The situation should improve now that *Stop Press*, a good program in its implementations on the Amstrad and BBC computers, is about to be published for the 64. At the moment, the best results can be obtained with the word processor that forms part of *GEOS*, a Macintosh–like icon–based operating environment for the Commodore 64, which also has the advantage of speeding up the disk drive. *GEOS* gives the ageing Commodore 64 a new lease of life.

Whatever your computer, you should be able to find software that will enable you to explore the fascination of desktop publishing. There are programs available even for such discontinued machines as the QL, and programs are in preparation for the new Sinclair Spectrum Plus Three, with its built–in disc drive.

Afterword

Desktop publishing makes available all sorts of possibilities to all sorts of people. It makes possible the existence of small publishing businesses, which are likely to be needed more and more as publishers amalgamate and take each other over, becoming part of vast world-wide conglomerates, whose business is promoting international best-sellers and who will have less time to nurture new, more fragile and less immediately profitable talents.

In such a world, which is now coming into being, writers can become their own printers and publishers. And those who have never thought of becoming writers can now do so, even if it is only on a family level. Instead of sending a Christmas card, try presenting family and friends with a well-presented and printed magazine of your year, or your life.

Businesses will need no encouragement to involve themselves in desktop publishing because they will appreciate that it cuts costs and speeds communication. Individuals, especially those who have regarded computers with suspicion, may need more persuading, until they discover that computers are creative, and that there are few aspects more creative than desktop publishing.

It will not be long before high street instant print shops are installing laser printers for customers' use. Soon, the cost of such printers will drop. Already, alternative and high-quality printing methods are being tested.

The price of computers and software not only falls, but the machines and the programs improve all the time. For anyone interested in words, in communication, in persuasion, desktop publishing provides as much enjoyment as you can find (while keeping your clothes on, anyway).

There is but one flaw. Desktop publishing software makes it easy for anyone to be be his or her own writer-printer-publisher; yet it ignores what could be regarded as the most important part of publishing: distribution.

It is essential, if you are trying to communicate something, to make sure that your words reach the right people. Distribution is often forgotten until it is too late, and a large pile of printed matter arrives on your doorstep with nowhere to go.

Fortunately, computers make distribution easier than it once was. Just as many newspapers now print in various regional centres in order to distribute

Afterword

copies quicker than if they came from one central point, so there may be times when it will be useful to have your publication printed in different parts of the country, or even the world.

Your original can be easily duplicated on to a floppy disk and put into the post for printing elsewhere. If, say, you were printing a newsletter for PageMaker users then you would not have to print it at all.

You could send a copy of your disc containing the finished pages to subscribers and let them load it into their *PageMaker* software and produce hard copy of it on whatever printer they had available.

It is also possible, providing you have a modem and suitable communications software, to transmit text and graphics over the telephone lines. Many, though, will have a captive audience, whether it is family, a community group or business colleagues.

William Morris, who created his own publishing house and designed the type, illustrations and decorations for the books it produced, wrote that "the chief source of art is man's pleasure in his daily necessary work, which expresses itself and is embodied in that art itself."

He added that the beauty of medieval handicrafts derived from the fact that the "workman had control over his material, tools and time."

Desktop publishing may not be necessary work for all, although it is obviously going to be an occupation for many graphic designers, but that beauty of being in control of a complete process is once again available to us. High tech meets medieval craft.

Professor Donald Knuth said the same thing in different words when interviewed by the American computer magazine *Byte* (February 1986).

"People just love to see something new that they can control and make words come out in a different way," he said. "This is lurking everywhere, and it is blossoming now because it's becoming available to people through less expensive machines all the time.

"So I know a revolution is coming."

Appendices & Index

Appendix A: Style book

There are two kinds of style book that a regular user of DTP software will need to keep. The first will list the fonts and typestyles to be used in a particular publication, in order to achieve consistency.

This will be a simple list, such as the following:

Text: 10/12 pt Times Roman (the second figure indicates the amount of leading, which in this instance would amount to two points.)
Headlines: 48 pt Helvetica for main headings.
Standfirst: 12 pt Helevetica.
Cross–headings: 12 pt Helvetica, set centered.
Captions: 10/12 Times Bold.

A style book might be far more elaborate than this example, depending upon the number of different fonts you use and your aim. For a newsletter, such a simple style would suffice, but for magazine you would probably use more display fonts and a greater variety of other typographical devices, ranging drop capitals to excerpts from the text set in larger type to break up the page and create eye–catching designs.

The other type of style book you need to maintain would concern words, where consistency is vitally important. Names must always be spelt in the same way throughout any publication and other matters of style, from abbreviations and titles of books or newspapers to the use of full points, need to display a similar uniformity.

A style book is best kept in a loose leaf folder so that additions to it can be made easily. A copy needs to be given to all contributors to a publication (although many are likely to ignore it). H. Hart's book *Rules for Compositors and Readers* (Oxford University Press), which has gone through umpteen editions, is a good starting point.

Nevertheless, such books cannot cover every eventuality, particularly for those who produce specialist publications dealing with all sorts of jargon. What follows is a brief example of the type of information you need to include, covering grammar, style and spelling. You will find, particularly in the early days of any publication, that new rulings will have to be made and added to the book every week.

Abbreviations: Do not use full point, eg "BBC" not "B.B.C." Do not use abbreviations for the first mention in copy of an organisation. Write "Department of Industry" first time and "DoI" on subsequent mentions.

Aim: People do not aim for things, they aim at them.

Ages: Give them, where necessary, after the name of the person, such as "Gandalf, 95".

Allergic: Refers to a bodily reaction, not to a dislike of something.

Apostrophes: They indicate possession and should always be written "'s". Write "Doris's", not "Doris'". They do not indicate plurals. The plural of "micros" is not "micro's".

Brand names: Avoid unless meant. It is "hard disk", not "Winchester".

Appendix A

Caddie: This is a golfing term. A caddy is a container for tea.

Collective nouns: They take singular verbs. "Apple is", not "Apple are".

Compare: Usually followed by "with". When it is followed by "to", it conveys a similarity rather than a difference.

Contractions: Avoid expressions such as "it's", unless saving space in a headline. "It is" is to be preferred. Do not abbreviate titles of rank or office. It is the Prime Minister, not the PM.

Decimals: They should have a 0 on numbers less than one. It is "0.5" not ".5".

Different: It is followed by "from", not "to". It should not be used to mean several.

First World War: Rather than World War I.

Flaunt: Do not confuse with "flout". Flaunt is to show off (if you've got it, flaunt it). Flout is to reject or mock.

Full point: They should not be used in abbreviations. It is Mr Clean, not Mr. Clean.

Inside: It should not be followed by "of". It is "inside the computer", not "inside of the computer".

–Ise: Use this spelling rather than –ize, as in "computerise".

It's: It's short for "it is" and is a contraction better avoided.

ITV: If you spell this out, refer to commercial television rather than to Independent Television.

Less: Avoid when referring to numbers. Use "fewer than".

Lowercase: It should be used for the seasons of the year. But write "Summer Time".

Names: Titles of programs, programmes, books, newspapers etc should be italicised.

Numbers: Spell out numbers up to nine, use figures for those higher.

Outside: It should not be followed by "of".

Over: Avoid when referring to numbers. Use "more than".

p: When this refers to money it should not be followed by a full point.

Second World War: Rather than World War II.

Short words: Use them whenever possible. Write "among", not "amongst", "hiccup", not "hiccough", "soon", not "in the near future".

Weights and measures: They should be abbreviated and kept to the singular. It is "lb" not "lbs", "km" not "kms".

Appendix B: Glossary

Agate: old term for five–and–a–half point type.

Ascender: the part of a letter that rises above the main body, as in the letters "b", "d", "f", "k", etc.

ASCII: American Standard Code for Information Interchange. A binary standard code of 128 characters, used in most microcomputers, to represent alphanumeric characters, punctuation marks and control codes.

Banner: the main headline of a newspaper, set across the full width of the page.

BASIC: acronym for Beginner's All–purpose Symbolic Instruction Code, the most popular computer language among amateur programmers.

Bastard measure: type set in a different width from the basic column width of a publication.

Binary: a numbering system that uses combinations of the digits 1 and 0 to represent its numbers.

Bit: short for binary digit, the basic unit of information used by a computer, which receives it as an electrical signal which is either a pulse, represented by a 1, or no pulse, represented a zero.

Bit–mapped display: a display that uses a specific location in memory for each pixel shown on the screen, providing high–quality images.

Black letter: type in the Germanic style, used for some newspaper titles and on Olde English tea–shoppes. Often called **Gothic** by those who do not care for it.

Bold: typeface which is thicker than the standard face.

Bleed: to place an illustration so that is continues over the margin to the edge of a page.

Body type: the type used for the main text of a publication.

Box: a section ruled off on four sides and containing either text or graphics.

Box–heading: a headline enclosed by rules or a border.

Brevier: old term for eight point type.

Bullet: blob at the beginning of a line of type to emphasise its importance.

Burgeois: old term for nine point type.

Business graphics: used in computing to mean charts and graphs or the software to produce charts and graphs.

Byline: a line of type containing the name of the author of a particular article.

Byte: the number of bits, usually eight, needed to represent a single alphanumeric character.

CAD: abbreviation for Computer Aided Design.

Camera–ready copy: a page of text or graphics ready to be converted to film as a stage in the process of phototypesetting. Known as CRC for short.

Caption: the explanatory text to an illustration.

Casting off: working out how much space a particular piece of copy will occupy in a particular type size.

Central Processing Unit: CPU for short. The microprocessor and circuits that interpret and execute the instructions.

Centred: type set so that it is placed in the middle of a line.

Character: an individual letter, number or punctuation mark.

Clip art: ready–made art, either printed or available on floppy disk, which then can be pasted into a publication. Computerised clip art can be resized easily before being electronically pasted into position.

Cock–up: initial letter set in a larger type than the accompanying matter and rising above the surrounding letters.

Column rule: rule used to separate columns of text, usually thin.

Condensed: type that is narrower than the standard face.

Copy: text, existing in manuscript or on floppy disk, that is ready for setting.

CP/M: short for Control Program/Monitor, it is a disk operating system which became the standard for 8–bit business computers, for which much software was written.

Crop: to cut down the size of an illustration or photograph.

Cross–head: a subheading set centered and inserted within the body of a text and referring to the following paragraph.

Cursive: type that imitates a handwritten style.

Cursor: an on–screen marker to show where the next chararacter will be typed.

Cut: to shorten an article, either for reasons of prolixity or to make it fit a given length.

Cut off: a rule across one or more columns of type.

Daisywheel printer: computer printer similar to an electric typewriter that can produce high–quality text but cannot print graphics. It is not compatible with desktop publishing software.

Data: the information stored and manipulated by a computer.

DDL: short for Document Design Language, a page description language used to control laser printers.

Deck: one line from a heading that occupies two lines or more.

Descender: that part of a letter which is below the body of the type, as in the letters "g", "j", "p", etc.

Desktop publishing: a means of publishing in which all stages, from writing to editing and type-setting are done by means of a personal computer using specialised software.

Digitiser: a means of converting data from analog to digital form and used in desktop publishing to capture photographic and television images and turn them into computer graphics.

Display type: the larger sizes of type used in headings.

Disk drive: a device for storing data that makes use of magnetic disks on which it records information. See **Floppy disk, Hard disk.**

Dot–matrix: computer printer which can print both text and graphics. It uses a pattern, or matrix, of dots, imprinted by needles hitting a ribbon, to form characters and graphics. In general, the more needles there are – 24 is the current maximum – then the better the quality of the print.

Dots per inch: often shortened to dpi, a measure of the density of print achieved with a printer.

Drop capital: an initial letter set in a larger type than the body text, covering two or more lines.

DTP: short for Desktop Publishing.

Dummy: used to describe both a detailed layout of a publication and a sample copy of a proposed publication.

EGA: short for Enhanced Graphics Adaptor, which is a card that plugs into an IBM PC in order to improve its graphics capability.

Egyptian typeface: See **Slab–serif.**

Elite: a type style which has 12 characters to the inch.

En: A space the size of a letter "n" used between words or as an indentation at the start of a paragraph. It is half an em. Also known as a **nut.**

English: old term for 14 point type.

Em: A space the size of a letter "m", which is as wide as it is high, used between words or as an indentation at the start of a paragraph. Also known as **mutton**, a term that normally refers to the 12 point m, which measures a pica.

Expanded: type that is broader than the standard face.

Face: see typeface.

Floppy disk: a plastic disk contained within a cardboard or plastic envelope on which computer programs and data are stored.

Flush left: used to describe text set flush with the left–hand margin of a page and with an uneven, or unjustified, right–hand margin.

Flush right: used to describe text set flush with the right–hand margin and with an uneven, or unjustified, left–hand margin.

Font: the entire set of alphanumeric type in one particular face and style.

Fount: see **Font**.

Freeze Frame: an image on a video recorder stopped on a single frame for prolonged viewing, which is a facility necessary for some digitisers to be able to digitise the image. See **Digitiser**.

Galley proof: a long strip of paper, containing a column or so of text, on which corrections are made in conventional printing before the text is made–up into a page.

GEM: short for Graphics Environment Manager, Digital Research's WIMP interface available for the IBM and compatible PCs and provided as standard on the Amstrad PC 1512 and the Atari ST. See **WIMP**.

Gothic: properly used to describe sans–serif typefaces, but also commonly applied to type in the German or Olde English style which is more correctly called **Black letter**.

Graphics: any illustrations created by means of a computer.

Graphics tablet: an electronically sensitive surface on which the user draws, using a stylus, puck or pencil, and the result appears on the screen.

Grotesque: often abbreviated to Grot and used to describe sans–serif type.

Gutter: the inner white space between a spread. See **Spread**.

Hanging indent: a paragraph with the first line set full out, and subsequent lines set a space – an em – in.

Hard copy: a printed version of words and pictures stored in the computer.

Hard disk: A rigid disk, which is normally sealed and not removable, that can store a vast amount of data and access it with great speed. They commonly come in 10, 20 and 40 Mbyte sizes.

Hard space: ensures that a group of words are not split.

Headline: the heading to an piece of writing, set in a display type.

Hyphenation: the splitting of a word, separated by a hyphen, over two lines, when text is set in columns. The ability of DTP software to break the word at the correct point.

Icon: a symbol on the screen that represents a program, a data file or an action, and which is activated by means of a pointer controlled by a mouse. See **Mouse, WIMP**.

Indent: setting that is less than the full column width. The command "nut each end", for example, means set the type an En in at each end of the line. Indentation is used when setting panels within copy or with paragraphs set in a different font in order to draw attention to them.

Inkjet: computer printer that squirts jets of ink through nozzles onto paper to form text or graphics. It is similar to a dot–matrix printer, but quieter and better at printing in colour.

Interpress: A page description language created at the Xerox Palo Alto Research Centre in America.

Italic: Roman typeface in which the letters are slanted to the right. It is harder to read and best used to give emphasis to words or paragraphs.

Justify: spacing lines or paragraphs of text to a given length so that both left– and right–hand margins are even.

K: short for kilobyte, a unit of measurement of the capacity of a computer's memory. One kilobyte equals 1024 bytes. For top quality desktop publishing, a computer with a minimum of 512K memory is needed. See **Byte**.

Kern: the overhanging part of a letter, which rests on the adjoining letter, such as the ascender and descender on an italic *f*. The spacing between such a letter and a following character needs careful adjustment, which is known as kerning.

Kerning: altering the amount of white space between letters.

Laser printer: computer printer capable of printing text and graphics to near typeset quality, using laser technology. Used to its best advantage in conjunction with a **page description language**.

Layout: the design for the arrangement of text and illustrations on a page.

Appendix B

Leading: adding space between lines of type, which makes it easier to read and is also a way of making copy which falls short fit a specified space.

Ligature: two or more letters combined on a single body in order that the spacing between them should be correctly adjusted. See **Kern.**

Light: typeface which is thinner than the regular face.

Lightpen: a photosensitive device, shaped like a pen, which can be used with some graphics software as a means of drawing. The user holds the pen so that it touches the monitor screen and the computer can register its movement.

Literal: a typographical error.

Long primer: old term for 10 point type.

Lower-case: the small letters in a font, as opposed to the capital, or upper-case, letters. The name derives from the cases, or small boxes, in which the metal type was kept. The small letters were kept in the lower case.

Mbyte: see **Megabyte.**

Make-up: putting type and illustrations into position on the page.

Margins: the blank edges to a page.

Measure: the length of a typeset line, usually expressed in picas.

Megabyte: unit of measurement of a computer's memory, equal to a million bytes.

Menu: a list of different actions that a particular program can perform, from which the user can choose one. The term is said to derive from choosing a meal by numbers from a Chinese restaurant menu. See **Pulldown menu.**

Minion: old term for seven point type.

Modem: formed from Modulator–Demodulator, it signifies a gadget to convert computer signals into a form that can be sent over telephone lines to another computer. It can be used to connect a personal computer to mainframe databases to discover information or to transfer data – from your computer to a typesetter, for instance.

Monitor: a screen, using a cathode ray tube, designed for computer displays and providing a higher quality image than a television set.

Mouse: a small object with a wheel underneath it and buttons on top which can be moved on a desktop to control the movement of a pointer on the screen. Part of the WIMP environment much used by DTP software.

Mutton: see em.

NLQ: initials standing for Near Letter Quality and used to describe dot-matrix printing which comes close to the output of daisywheel printers.

Nonpareil: old term for 6 point type. Used as a unit of measurement, since it equals half a pica em.

Nut: see en.

Orphan: a word on its own at the top of a column or a page of text. Orphans are ugly. See **Widow.**

Outline: a type-style in which the characters are drawn in outline only so that they are made up of a black line enclosing white space.

Over-matter: copy that has been set but not used in a publication.

Page Description Language: computer language used to describe a page of text or graphics to a laser printer. The best known PDL is **PostScript.**

Pagination: the numbering of pages in a publication, a process that some software carries out automatically.

Paste-up: complete copy of a publication, with text and illustrations pasted in positions.

PDL: see **page description language.**

Pearl: old term for five point type.

Pica: old term for 12 point type. A pica em, which is 12 x 12 points, is used as a measure indicating the width of a column of a type and is one of the units of measurement to be found in desktop publishing systems. It is equal precisely to a sixth of an inch in desktop publishing, and approximately in conventional printing.

Pica type: a type style which has ten characters to the inch.

Pixel: picture element, or one of the dots that form a picture on a television or monitor screen.

Plotter: a printer that uses a pen or pens to draw on paper computer–created graphics, such as graphs, charts and architectural plans.

Point: unit of measurement for the size of type. There are precisely 72 points to an inch in desktop publishing, and approximately in conventional printing. In most publications, type sizes will range from 5 to 12 points for the setting of text and from 14 points to 72 points for the setting of headlines.

PostScript: Page Description Language to control the output of laser printers. **PostScript** is the nearest to the standard, having been endorsed by both Apple and IBM for use with their desktop publishing systems.

Printer driver: a program that instructs a printer how to provide hard copy of data, such as text and graphics, stored in a computer's memory.

Program: see **software**.

Pulldown menu: a list of actions that a particular program can perform which appears when the user moves a mouse–controlled pointer to the top of the screen display. One can be chosen by moving the pointer to it and clicking on a mouse–button. Much used by DTP software.

Ragged left: type set with a ragged lefthand margin and an even right one.

Ragged right: type set with a ragged righthand margin and an even left one.

RAM: short for Random Access Memory, the amount of a computer's internal memory available to hold programs and data. The contents of the memory are lost when the computer is switched off. See **ROM**.

Rejig: to make changes to copy that has been set.

Resolution: the quality of screen display, which is dependent upon the number of pixels used. The higher, the better.

Reverse indent: see **hanging indent**.

RIP: Raster Image Processor, which turns the code provided by a Page Description Language into pulses to control the laser beam used in a laser printer. See **PDL, Laser printer**.

ROM: short for Read Only Memory, which is contained in pre–programmed chips in the computer. It cannot be altered, nor is it affected by switching off the computer.

Roman: elegant serif typeface in which the letters are made up of tick and thin strokes. Over the centuries the shape has moved away from a style similar to handwriting with slanted serifs to one closer to engraving, with vertical serifs.

Ruby: old term for five–and–a–quarter point type.

Rules: dividing lines between columns of text.

Running head: descriptive line that appears at the top of every page of a publication.

Sans–serif: typefaces that lack serifs, those little flourishes or brackets at the ends of letters. It is a style better suited to headings than to body–text.

Scaling: changing the size of an illustration.

Scanner: machine that can turn text or an illustration into digitised form so that it can be loaded into a computer.

Screen dump: a printed version of screen images; or the software required to produce one.

Serif: typeface that has little flourishes at the end of letters. The best–known serif faces are Roman and Italic. Roman is the type best suited for body–text and is also an effective display typeface.

Shadow: a type–style in which the characters cast a shadow.

Sidehead: subheading contained within a body of text, set flush left, and referring to the paragraph that follows it.

Slab Serif: Heavy Victorian typeface with square serifs. Also known as **Egyptian**.

Soft hyphenation: hyphenation where the user adds hyphens to words so that they will be correctly broken when they fall at the end of a line of type and are too long to fit the available space.

Appendix B

Software: a computer program, or series of instructions to the computer to carry out certain actions.

Solid matter: type set without leading.

Spread: two facing pages which form the basic unit of design for most publications.

Small Caps: capital letters of the same size as lower-case letters.

Strapline: headline set over the main headline, in smaller type.

Thermal printer: computer printer with heating elements that can produce an image on special paper. They are quiet in use, but otherwise have nothing in their favour.

Thick lead: a wide space of 3 points between lines of type, or an instruction to a printer to put a thick lead between the lines. See **leading**.

Thin lead: a small space, usually 1 point, between lines of type, or an instruction to a printer to put a thin lead between the lines. See **leading**.

Trackball: gadget akin to a mouse and sometimes used as a replacement for one. It contains a ball a little smaller than a tennis ball mounted within a flat case. By rolling the ball with fingers or palm within its mounting, the user can control the movement of an on-screen pointer. Trackballs are sensitive devices that can be used to control some art and CAD programs.

Typeface: a particular style of type.

Type style: type in a specific style, such as bold, condensed, italic, outline or shadow.

Unjustified: text in which the lines are of an irregular length.

Upper-case: the capital letters of a font.

Upgrade: to improve the capabilities of a computer or software; to move from one version of a program to a later, better one. Some DTP software has reached its third version.

White space: term for the space on a page not occupied by printing.

Widow: A short line which ends a paragraph. Widows at the bottom or top of a column or a page of text should be avoided. See **Orphan**.

WIMP: acronym for Windows, Icons, Mouse, Pointer (or, if you prefer Windows, Icons, Mouse, Pulldown Menus), the graphics-based interface between a user and a computer's operating system made fashionable by Apple's Macintosh computer. It is part of most desktop publishing systems.

Window: a section of the screen, marked off by a frame, which can display data such as document being edited within a word processor. Opening several windows on a screen would enable the user to see different parts of the same document or different documents and to transfer information between them.

WYSIWIG: acronym for What You See Is What You Get, meaning that the printed version of your publication will be the same as what you see on the monitor screen.

X-height: the height of a character of type, measured by the lowercase "x", which lacks ascenders and descenders.

Appendix C: Reference

What follows is not intended as a comprehensive guide to available products, since that would require another book, particularly for IBM PC and Macintosh software and hardware. Manufacturers or distributors of products mentioned in the text are listed, together with other useful hardware and software and suggestions of some books for further reading and inspiration. It is organised for the most part by computer. Word processing programs are listed only if they include some desktop publishing functions, such as the integration of text and graphics, or setting text in columns, or the use of different fonts within a document. The names and addressess of the publishers or of leading distributors are provided in case your local dealer, always the best place to begin looking, does not have the product.

AMSTRAD CPC
DTP Software
Stop Press: Advanced Memory Systems.
Magazine Maker: includes **Stop Press** and **Rombo Vidi** video digitiser. Advanced Memory Systems.
Fleet Street Editor: Mirrorsoft.

Fonts, Clip Art & Ready-to-use Graphics
Extra! Extra!: clip art for use with **Stop Press**. Advanced Memory Systems.

Graphics Sofware
AMX Mouse: mouse and art program. Advanced Memory Systems.
DR Graph: business graphics. Digital Research.
DR Draw: Digital Research.
Microdraft: CAD. Timatic Systems.

Print Enhancers
Font64: font designer for output to Amstrad or Epson compatible dot matrix printers. Hisoft.
Print Master: font designer, fonts and screen dump for DMP 2000 and Epson compatible dot matrix printers. Siren Technology.
Scriptor: six character fonts for use with DMP1 printer. Pride Utilities.
Tasprint 464: five fonts for dot matrix printer output, compatible with **Amsword** and **Tasprint** word processors. Tasman Software.

Video & Graphics Hardware
Dart Scanner: Dart Electronics.
Linscan: works in conjunction with Plotmate plotter. Linear Graphics Ltd.
Video Digitiser: John Morrison.
Vidi: digitiser. Rombo Productions.

AMSTRAD PCW
DTP Software
The Desktop Publisher: Database Software.
DocuMentor: Python Microsystems.
Fleet Street Editor Plus: Mirrosoft.
Newsdesk International: The Electric Studio.
Stop Press: Advanced Memory System.

Fonts, Clip Art & Ready-to-use Graphics
Fonts 'n' Graphics: for use with **Fleet Street Editor Plus**. Mirrorsoft.

Graphics Software
DR Draw: Digital Research..
DR Graph: business graphics. Digital Research.
Powercad: CAD. Grafsales Ltd.

Print Enhancers
Flexitype: 40 fonts for use with Epson or compatible dot matrix printers. Kenilworth Computers.
Supertype: eight typefaces compatible with **Locoscript** word processor. Digita.
Tasprint 800: fonts for use with **Tasword 800** word processor. Tasman Software

Reference

Video & Graphics Hardware
Grafpad II: graphics tablet. Grafsales Ltd. .
Light Pen: pen, compatible with **DR Draw**, and art program. Electric Studio.
Linscan: works in conjunction with Plotmate plotter. Linear Graphics Ltd.
Video Digitiser: Electric Studio.
Vidi: digitiser. Rombo Productions.

ATARI ST
DTP Software
Fleet Street Publisher: Mirrorsoft.
Publishing Partner: Silica Shop Ltd.

Document Processing Software
Calligrapher: Computer Concepts.
1st Word Plus: Electric Software.
Signum: HB Marketing Ltd.

Fonts, Clip Art & Ready-to-use Graphics
PaintPro Library 1: clip art and fonts for use with **PaintPro**. Abacus Software.

Graphics Software
Art Director: Mirrorsoft.
CAD 3D: Electric Software.
Degas Elite: Ariolasoft.
PaintPro: Abacus Software.
K–Graph 2: business graphics. Kuma.

Print Enhancer
Megafont ST: XLent Software.

Video & Graphics Hardware
Haba Video Digitiser: HB Marketing.
Pro–Draw Graphics Tablet: Eidersoft Software Ltd.

BBC B/B+/MASTER/MASTER COMPACT
DTP Software
Admin Extra: utilities for use with **Fleet Street Editor**. Mirrorsoft.
Fleet Street Editor: Mirrorsoft.
Magazine Maker: includes **Stop Press** and **Beeb Video Digitiser**. Watford Electronics.
Stop Press: Advanced Memory Systems.
Typesetter: Sherston Software.

Fonts, Clip Art & Ready-to-use Graphics
Clipboard Graphics Library: for use with **Stop Press**. Micro Studio.
Extra! Extra!: clip art fonts and utilities for **Stop Press**. Advanced Memory Systems.
Fonts 'n' Graphics: for use with **Fleet Street Editor**. Mirrorsoft.
Walt Disney Graphics: for use with **Fleet Street Editor**. Mirrorsoft.

Graphics Software
AB2: AB Designs.
AMX Superart: Advanced Memory Systems.
Diagram: CAD. Pineapple Software
Diagram Utilities: Pineapple Software.
Graphito: graphics programming system. Addison–Wesley Ltd.
Hersey Characters: font generator. Beebugsoft.
Interactive 3D: CAD. Design Dynamics.
Inter–Chart: business graphics, compatible with **Inter–Sheet** spreadsheet. Computer Concepts.
Novacad: CAD. Technomatic.
Quest: mouse and art program, compatible with **Beeb video digitiser**. Watford Electronics.
3D Graphics Development System: Glentop Publishing.
Viewplot: business graphics. Acornsoft.

Print Enhancers
Fontaid: 40 fonts and font designer for Canon and Kaga NLQ dot matrix printers. CJE Micro's.
Fontaid A–C: more fonts for use with **Fontaid**. CJE Micro's.
Fontwise Plus: fonts and font editor for Epson and compatible dot–matrix printers. Clares.

MF–B: 12 fonts for use with Multi–Font NLQ. CJE Micro's.
MF–C: 15 fonts for use with Multi–Font NLQ. CJE Micro's.
Multi–Font NLQ: user definable fonts for most dot matrix printers. CJE Micro's.
NLQ Designer: downloadable font designer for Kaga KP810-910 and Canon PW1080 dot matrix printers. Watford Electronics.
PMS Multifonts NTQ: for Epson and compatible dot-matrix printers. Includes font editor. PMS.
Signwriter: font designer and printer of characters at any size. Wight Scientific.

Video & Graphics Hardware
Beeb Video Digitiser: Watford Electronics.
Grafpad II: graphics tablet. Grafsales Ltd.
Linscan: scanner, works in conjunction with **Plotmate** plotter. Linear Graphics Ltd.
MicroEye: scanner. Digithurst Ltd.
Polaroid Palette: allows production of 35mm slides direct from the screen. Polaroid (UK) Ltd.

COMMODORE AMIGA
DTP Software
City Desk: PostScript compatible. MicroSearch Inc.
PageSetter: Gold Disk Software.
PageSetter LaserScript: PostScript laser printer driver for **PageSetter**, with Courier, Helvetica, Symbol and Times fonts. Gold Disk
Professional Page: supports Amiga's colour capabilities. Gold Disk.
Publisher 1000: Brown–Wagh Publishing.
Shakespeare: for colour printing, includes graphic design templates. Infinity.

Document Processing Software
ProWrite: Text and graphics in colour. New Horizons Software.
Vizawrite: Viza Software.

Fonts, Clip Art & Ready–to–use Graphics
Aegis Art Pack 1: Clip art for **Aegis Images**. Precision Software Ltd.
Aegis Art Pack 2: Clip art for **Aegis Images**. Precision Software Ltd.
Desktop Artist: Clip art for **City Desk**. MicroSearch Inc.
DPaint Art: Clip art and utilities for **Deluxe Paint**. Electronic Arts.
Font-a-Size: utility to scale Amiga fonts to any size. Earthbound Software.
Fonts: library of fonts. Earthbound Software.
JetSet: Hewlett Packard Laserjet or compatible printer driver. C Ltd.
FontSet1: dot-matrix printer fonts for use with **PageSetter**. Gold Disk.
JetSet Fonts: downloadable fonts for Hewlett Packard LaserJet printer. C Ltd.
LaserFonts1: three downloadable fonts for LaserWriter use. S. Anthony Studios.
TV Text: text manipulation. Brown–Wagh Publishing.
Zuma Fonts, Vols 1–3: each volume contains three display fonts in six sizes. Brown–Wagh Publishing

Graphics Software
Aegis Draw: CAD. Precision Software Ltd.
Aegis Images: Precision Software Ltd. .
Aegis Impact: business graphics. Precision Software Ltd.
DeluxePaint II: Electronic Arts.
Digi–Paint: allows use of Amiga's 4096 colour for manipulation of **Digi–View** images. Newtek Inc.
Dynamic–CAD: CAD. Microillusions.
LaserUp! Graphics: print utility for use with LaserWriter printer. S. Anthony Studios.

Writing Aid
Reason: proofreader and style analyser. The Other Guys.

Print Enhancers
Fine-Font: for Epson and compatible dot–matrix printers. Earthbound Software.
Fine-Fonts: library of fonts for use with Fine–Font. Earthbound Software.

Video & Graphics Hardware
Cherry A3 Graphic Tablet: Precision Software.
Digi–View: digitiser. 640 x 400 resolution with 128 gray levels. NewTek.
Easyl: graphics pad. Anakin Research.
Penmouse Plus: graphics pad. Kurta Corp.

Appendix C

Polaroid Palette: allows production of 35mm slides direct from the screen. Polaroid UK.
Pro–Draw Graphics Tablet: graphics pad. Eidersoft Software.

COMMODORE 64/128
DTP Software
Newsroom: Ariolasoft.
Stop Press: Advanced Memory Systems.

Document Processing Software
Writers Workshop: includes **GeoWrite, Text Grabber, GeoLaser** for LaserWriter printer compatibility. Requires **Geos**, a WIMP environment. First Analytical.

Fonts, Clip Art & Ready–to–use Graphics
Font Pack 1: for use with Geowrite. First Analytical.
Newsroom Clip Art 1: Ariolasoft.
Newsroom Clip Art 2: Ariolasoft.

Graphics Software
Art Studio: Rainbird Software.
B Graph: business graphics. Ariolasoft.
Chartpak: business graphics. Precision Software.
CADPAK: business graphics for use with plotter. Precision Software.
The Image System: CRL.

Video & Graphics Hardware
Computereyes: digitiser. Precision Software.
Koala Pad: graphics pad. Precision Software.

IBM PC and COMPATIBLES
Complete Desktop Publishing Systems
Apricot: Includes Apricot Xen–i 386 IBM compatible computer, **PageMaker** software and Apricot Laser printer.
AST Europe: Includes IBM compatible computer, AST Turboscan scanner and AST TurboLaser printer.
Canon: Personal Publishing System includes Canon IBM compatible computer, Canon Image Scanner, Canon laser printer.
Rank Xerox: Documenter system consists of the 6085 Professional Computer, the 4045 Laser Copier/Printer and **VP Local Laser** software.

DTP Programs
ETG Desktop Publishing System; DAK Industries.
Finesse: Advanced Memory Systems.
Fleet Street Editor: Mirrorsoft.
Fontasy: Ctrl Alt Deli.
Fontasy Toolkit: utilities for Fontasy. Ctrl Alt Deli.
FrontPage: Postscript compatible. Studio Software.
GEM Desktop Publisher: incorporates **1st Word Plus** word processing software. Digital Research.
Harvard Professional Publisher: PostScript compatible. Software Publishing Europe.
PageMaker 2.0: PostScript compatible. Aldus.
Spellbinder: PostScript compatible. Lexisoft.
Ventura Publisher: PostScript compatible. Rank Xerox UK.

Document Processing Software
Manuscript: Lotus.
Samna Word IV: Samna.
Word 3.1: Microsoft.
Wordcraft Elite: Wordcraft.
WordPerfect 4.2: Sentinel Software.
XyWrite III: Xyquest.

Fonts, Clip Art & Ready–to–use Graphics
Fontasy Font Packs, Vol 1–3: extra fonts for use with **Fontasy**. Ctrl Alt Deli.
Gem Font Editor: for use with **GEM**. Digital Research.
Gem Fonts: for use with **GEM**. Digital Research.
MyFont: Software City.

Graphics Software
The Art Studio: Mirrorsoft.
AutoCAD: CAD. Autodesk.
AutoSketch: low–cost CAD. Autodesk.
Chart 2.0: business graphics. Microsoft.
Freelance Plus: business graphics. Lotus.
GEM Draw: Digital Research.
GEM Graph: business graphics. Digital Research.
Harvard Presentation Graphics: business graphics. Software Publishing Europe.
PC Paintbrush: ZSoft Corpn.
PC–Slide: business graphics for computer generated slides. Management Graphics.
Powercad: CAD. Grafsales.

Print Enhancers
Fancy Font: font designer and high quality slow–printing fonts. SoftCraft.
Flexitype: 40 fonts for use with Epson or compatible dot matrix printers. Kenilworth Computers.
Fontastic: novelty fonts. IHS Systems.
LePrint: for use with WordStar files. Writing Consultants.
Lettrix: memory resident fonts and font designer. Ideal Software Ltd.
NicePrint: memory resident serif fonts. Spies Laboratories.
Printworks: small and foreign language fonts. SoftStyle.
Tasprint PC: font designer and 20 print styles for use with dot matrix printers. Tasman Software.
Tech/Print: graphics and foreign language fonts for use with WordStar. Goldstein Software.
TypeFaces: display fonts.

Typesetting Software
Deskset: GB Techniques.
Do–It: Studio Software.
LaserMaker: Lasermaker.
MicroTEX: Addison–Wesley.
Newswriter: Cognita.
PC TEX: Personal TEX.
Printworks: memory resident driver for laser printers. P & P Micro Distributors.
ScenicWriter: Scenic Computer Systems.
SuperPage: Bestinfo.

Writing Aids
Grammatik: style analyser. Raven Computer.
Rightwriter: style analyser. Decisionware.

Large Screen Monitors
ETAP Monitor: ETAP.
MegaScreen II: Thames Valley Systems; Computers Unlimited.
Laserview: Appropriate Technology.
Monitherm Viking 1: Appropriate Technology.
Wyse 700: Wyse Technology.

Video & Graphics Hardware
Computereyes: digitiser. Precision Software.
Cherry Graphics Tablet: Cherry Electrical Products.
Dest PC Scan: Formscan.
Grafpad II: graphics tablet. Grafsales.
Linscan: works in conjunction with **Plotmate** plotter. Linear Graphics.
MicroEye: scanner. Digithurst.
Microsight: scanner. Digithurst.
Polaroid Palette: allows production of 35mm slides direct from the screen. Polaroid.
ReadRight: scanner. Canon.
SummaSketch: graphics tablet. Summagraphics.

MACINTOSH
Complete Desktop Publishing System
Apple: Includes Macintosh computer, **PageMaker** software, LaserWriter printer.

DTP Software
ComicWorks: Mirrorsoft.
GraphicWorks: Mirrorsoft.

Appendix C

MacPublisher III: PostScript compatible. Boston Publishing Systems.
PageMaker: PostScript compatible. Aldus.
PageMaker Portfolio: contains 21 formats for newsletters for use with **PageMaker**. Aldus.
Ragtime: P & P Micro Distributors.
Ready Set Go 3.0: PostScript compatible. Esselte Letraset.
Typecast: Unified Technology.
XPress: for colour printing. Heyden & Son.

Document Processing Software
MacAuthor: Icon Technology.
MacWrite: Apple Computer (UK) Ltd.
Word 3.0: Microsoft.
WriteNow: T/Maker Company.

Fonts, Clip Art & Ready−to−use Graphics
Adobe Systems' Type Library: selection of downloadable typefaces for use with any PostScript compatible printer or typesetter: Aldus UK Ltd.
Art File: illustrations designed for the British market. Forest Marketing.
Business Forms: more than 40 ready−to−use forms. MacSoft.
Desktop Art: collection of clip art designed for use with the LaserWriter and so far comprising: **Artfolio 1, Education 1, Graphics & Symbols 1, Four Seasons 1, Sport 1**. Dynamic Graphics.
Display Fonts: selection of unusual fonts. MacSoft.
Fluent Fonts: screen and laser font designer. The MacSerious Company.
Fontographer:laser−font editor. The MacSerious Company.
Gallery: selection of pictures, borders, maps. MacSoft.
GhostFonts: allows backgrounded or shaded fonts on LaserWriter and LaserWriter Plus. MacSoft.
GreyFonts: allows printing of shaded type with LaserWriter.
Hands: includes food, leisure, tradesmen. MacSoft.
Instant UK Atlas: maps. MacSoft.
Laser Forms: business forms stored as **MacDraw** files. MacSoft.
LaserWorks V1.2: font and character designer for use with LaserWriter. DOS (Europe).
MacForms: business forms compatible with **MacPaint**. Datafood Software Company.
Page Forms: business forms formatted in the Master page of **PageMaker**. MacSoft.
SoftForms: business forms compatible with **MacPaint**. Artsci Inc.
Symbols: selection of animal, farming, tourist symbols etc. MacSoft.
TextEffects: manipulates text for use with LaserWriter. McQueen.

Graphics Software
ClickArt Effects: adds manipulative routines to MacPaint. T/Maker.
Cricket Draw: generates PostScript Code. Heyden & Son.
Cricket Graph: for graphs and charts. Heyden & Son Ltd.
FullPaint: McQueen.
Illustrator: Aldus UK Ltd.
MacDraft: Microspot.
MacDraw: Apple Computer UK Ltd.
MacPaint: Apple Computer UK Ltd.
SuperPaint: The MacSerious Company.

Typesetting Software
JustText: MacEurope.
MacTEX: FTL Systems.
TEXtures: version of TEX. Addison−Wesley.
TypoMac: Serif Software.

Writing Aid
MacProof: Mayfield.

Large−Screen Monitors
MegaScreen II: Thames Valley Systems; Computers Unlimited.
Radius Full Page Display: McQueen Ltd.

Video & Graphics hardware
Abaton Scanners: range of six scanners. Applied Technology Marketing.
JustText Scanner: MacEurope.
Macintizer: graphic tablet. SSI.

MacScan: Heyden & Son.
MacVision: digitiser. Koala Technologies.
Magic: Heyden & Son.
MegaScan: Megabyte.
Microtek MS–300A Scanner: McQueen Ltd.
Neotech Video Scanner: for grabbing video images. ARS Microsystems.
Private Eye: digitiser. I/O Video.
Thunderscan: scanner. Thunderware Inc.

QL

I've never used a QL for desktop publishing and don't intend to try. For those that have one and want to, there is a limited range of software available.
DTP Software
Desktop Publisher: works with Epson compatible dot matrix printers. Digital Precision.
Front Page: works with Epson compatible dot matrix printers. GAP Software.

Graphics Program
Eye–Q: Digital Precision.

Print Enhancer
Q Writer: TK Computerware.

PRINTERS
Laser Printer Manufacturers/Distributors
AES Data UK Ltd., 24 Gt. Pulteney St., London W1 (Tel:01–439 4272).
British Olivetti Ltd., First Avenue, Bletchley, Milton Keynes MK1 1RL. (Tel: 0908–749000).
Canon (UK) Ltd., Canon House, Manor Rd., Wallington, Surrey SM6 0AJ. (Tel 01–773 3173).
Centronics Data Computer (UK) Ltd., Petersham House, Harrington Rd., London SW7 3HA. (Tel: 01–581 1011).
C. Itoh Ltd., Beacon House, 26/28 Worple Rd., Wimbledon, London SW19 4EE. (Tel: 01–946 4960).
Citizen Europe Ltd. Wellington House, 4/10 Cowley Rd., Uxbridge, Middlesex UB8 2XW. (Tel: 0895–72621). (Tel: 0895 72621).
Dataproducts Ltd., Dataproducts House, 136–138 High St., Egham, Surrey TW20 9HL. (Tel: 0734–31161).
Epson (UK) Ltd., Dorland House, 388 High Rd., Wembley, Middlesex. (Tel: 01–902 8892).
Facit Ltd., Maidstone Rd., Rochester, Kent ME1 3QN. (Tel:0634 401721).
Genicom International Ltd., Unit B1, The Summit Centre, Summit Avenue, Southwood, Nr. Farnborough, Hampshire GU14 0LU. (Tel: 0252–521555).
Kyocera: Mekom Computer Products Ltd., Enfield Hall, Enfield Rd., Edgbaston, Birmingham B15 1QA.
Hewlett–Packard Ltd., Miller House, The Ring, Bracknell, Berkshire RG12 1XN. (Tel: 0344–424898).
Oki: Trinitec plc, Unit 6, Bittacy Business Centre, Bittacy Hill, London NW7 1BA. (Tel: 01–349 1111).
Mannesmann Talley, Molly Millars Lane, Wokingham, Berkshire RG11 2QT. (Tel: 0734–788711).
NEC Business Systems (Europe) Ltd., 35 Oval Rd., Camden Town, London NW1 7EA. (Tel: 01–267 7000).
Qume (UK) Ltd., Qume House, Park Way, Newbury, Berkshire RG13 1EE. (Tel: 0635–31400)
Rank Xerox UK, Bridge House, Oxford Rd., Uxbridge, Middlesex UB8 1HS. (Tel:0895–51133).
Siemens, St. Catherine's House, 2 Hanworth Rd., Feltham, Middlesex TW13 5BA. (Tel: 0932–785691).
Texas Instruments Ltd., Manton Lane, Bedford MK41 7PA. (Tel: 0234 27011).
Wenger Printers Ltd., Unit 10, The Valley Centre, Gordon Rd., High Wycombe. (Tel:0494 450941).
Xitan/LaserMaster UK, Xitan House, 27 Salisbury Rd., Totton, Southampton. (Tel: 0703–871211).

24–Pin Dot–Matrix Printer Manufacturers/Distributors
Brother Office Equipment, Jones & Brother, Shepley St., Audenshaw, Manchester M34 5JD. (Tel: 061–330 6531).
C.Itoh Ltd.
Citizen Europe Ltd.
Epson (UK) Ltd.
Fujitsu Europe Ltd., Royal Trust House, 54 Jermyn St., SW1Y 6NQ. (Tel: 01–408 0043).

Appendix C

NEC Business Systems.
Printronix, Park Rd., Rhosymede, Wrexham, Clwyd LL14 3YR. (Tel: 0978–823321).
Mannesmann Talley.
Star Micronics UK Ltd., Craven House, 40 Uxbridge Rd., London W5 2BS. (Tel: 01–840 1800).
Toshiba Information Systems (UK) Ltd., International House, Windmill Rd., Sunbury on Thames, Middlesex TW16 7HR. (Tel: 0932 785666).

Colour Thermal Head Printers
Mitsubishi G500: resolution of 240 dpi.
Mitsubishi G650: resolution of 300 dpi. **Mitsubishi Electric UK Ltd.**, Hertford Place, Maple Cross, Rickmansworth, Herts WD3 2BJ. (Tel: 0923–770000).

TYPESETTING BUREAUX
Companies specialising in typesetting from microcomputer discs and desktop publishing software.
Align Design, London House, 26–40 Kensington High St., London W8.
AppleCentre, Second City Systems Ltd., Second City House, Warwick Rd., Birmingham B11 2EW. (Tel: 021–707 8739).
Bit 32 Ltd., 32 North John St., Liverpool L2 9QJ. (Tel:051–227 3232).
Budget Typesetting, 53 Rowan Walk, Bromley, Kent BR2 8QW. (Tel:0689 53546).
The Computer Graphics Factory, 1 Elystan Place, Chelsea, London SW3. (Tel:01–581 3556).
Cotswold Press Ltd., Stanton Harcourt Rd., Eynsham, Oxford. (Tel:0865–880608)
Inprint Ltd., 39 Chiltern St., London W1M 1HJ. (Tel:01–935 7140).
McNicol Datacom Ltd., Unit 9, Hazelwood Trading Estate, Worthing, Sussex BN14 8NP. (Tel:0903–210646).
P's & Q's, 18 Harrington St., Liverpool L2 9QA. (Tel:051–236 7953).
Wordsmiths, 33 Clerkenwell Close, London EC1R 0AU. (Tel:01–608 1868).

USER GROUPS & PUBLIC DOMAIN SOFTWARE SUPPLIERS
User groups are an excellent source of information and help. Most charge a moderate subscription; some, such as ICPUG, are run by enthusiasts, others are commercial enterprises. Many supply at a low cost public domain software, which can be a cheap source of printing utilities and other useful programs.
Advantage, 33 Malyns Close, Chinnor, Oxfordshire, OX9 4EW. (Tel: 0844 52075). PD library for Amstrad CPC and PCW, and IBM PC.
Amiga Users Group (UK), 66 London Rd., Leicester LE2 0QD. (Tel: 0533–550993). PD library of more than 50 disks.
AmigaWorld PD Library, 80 Elm St., Peterborough, NH 03458, USA. (Tel: 603–924 9471). Bi-monthly magazine maintains a national PD library for the Amiga.
Beebug, PO Box 109, High Wycombe, Bucks. HP10 8HQ. Publisher of a monthly magazine for BBC users full of useful programs that are also available on disc and tape.
CPM/UG, 72 Mill Rd., Hawley, Dartford, Kent. PD library of CP/M software.
The 1512 Independent User Group, PO Box 55, Sevenoaks, Kent, TN13 1 AQ. PD library of more than 400 disks for the Amstrad PC.
IBM PC User Group, PO Box 830, London SE1 2BQ. (Tel: 01–232 2277). PD library of more than 240 disks.
Independent Commodore Producers User Group (ICPUG), Membership Secretary, 30 Brancaster Rd., Newbury Park, Ilford, Essex 1G2 7EP. PD libraries for Amiga, Commodore PC, Commodore 64, Commodore 128 (including CP/M).
Macintosh User Group UK, 55 Linkside Ave., Oxford OX2 8JE. PD library.
MCSoft, 9 Abingdon Gardens, Bath, Avon BA2 2UY. PD library for the Atari ST.
PC–SIG Software Library, 90 Braybourne Close, Uxbridge, Middlesex UB8 1UJ. (Tel: 0895 51978). PD library of IBM software.
ST Users' Club, 52 Mimosa St., London SW6 4DT. PD library.

BOOKS
Alphabets and Ornaments, by Ernest Lehner (Dover Publications, 1968).
The Alternative Printing Handbook, by Chris Trewerk and Jonathan Zeitlyn (Penguin Books, 1983).
Art Deco Alphabets, a Treasury of Original Alphabets from the 1920s and 1930s, compiled by Frederick S. Copley (The Main Street Press, 1985)
Art Deco Display Alphabets, selected and arranged by Dan X. Solo (Dover Publications, 1982).
Basic Typography, by John R. Biggs (Faber and Faber, 1968).
The Design Concept, by Allen Hurlburt (Watson–Guptill, 1981).
Desktop Publishing: Using PageMaker on the Apple Macintosh, by Andrew Lucas (Ellis Horwood, 1987).

The Encyclopedia of Type Faces, by W. Pincus Jaspert, W. Turner Berry, A.F. Johnson (Blandford Press, 1970).
Editing and Design, Volumes 1-5, by Harold Evans (William Heinemann, 1973-1978).
Fantastic Alphabets, created by Jean Larcher (Dover Publications, 1976).
The Graphics of Communication, by Arthur Turnbull and Russell N. Baird (Holt, Rinehart and Winston, Inc., 1968).
Handbook of Pictorial Symbols, by Rudolph Modley and W. R. Myers (Dover Publications, 1980).
Layout: the design of the printed page, by Allen Hurlburt (Watson-Guptill, 1977).
Lettercraft, by John R. Biggs (Blandford Press, 1982).
Letter Forms, by Stanley Morison (Nattali & Maurice, 1968).
The Making of Books, by Sean Jennett (Faber & Faber, 1973).
Modern English Usage, by H. W. Fowler (Oxford University Press, 1957).
Modern Display Alphabets, edited by Paul E. Kennedy (Dover Publications, 1978).
Newspaper Design, by Allen Hutt (Oxford University Press, 1960).
On Type Designs Past And Present, by Stanley Morison (Ernest Benn, 1962).
Original Art Deco Designs, by William Rowe (Dover Publications, 1973).
Ornamental Alphabets and Initials, by Alison Harding (Thames and Hudson, 1983).
PostScript Language Tutorial and Cookbook (Addison-Wesley, 1985).
PostScript Language Reference Manual (Addison-Wesley, 1985).
Printing Types: Their History, Forms and Use, Volumes 1-2, by Daniel Berkeley Updike (Dover Publications, 1970).
Special Effects and Topical Alphabets, selected and arranged by Dan X. Solo (Dover Publications, 1978).
Techniques of Typography, by Cal Swann (Lund Humphries, 1965).
The TEX Book, by Donald Knuth (Addison Wesley, 1984).
Treasury of Alphabets and Lettering, by Jan Tschichold (Omega Books, 1985).
Treasury of Authentic Art Nouveau Alphabets, Decorative Initials, Monograms, Frames and Ornaments, edited by Ludwig Petzendorfer (Dover Publications, 1984).
Type For Books: A Designer's Manual, (Bodley Head for Mackays, 1976).
Typographic Design, by Raymond Roberts, (Ernest Benn, 1966).
The Typography of Press Advertisements, by Kenneth Day, (Ernest Benn Ltd., 1956).
Understanding Media, by Marshall McLuhan (Routledge and Kegan Paul, 1964).
Usage and Abusage: A Guide to Good English, by Eric Partridge (Hamish Hamilton, 1965).

MAGAZINES & NEWSLETTERS
DTP Desktop Publishing: Dennis Publishing Ltd., 14 Rathbone Place, London W1P 1DE. (Tel: 01-631 1433).
Desktop Publisher: The Desktop Publishing Company, Hithermoor Rd., Stanwell Moor, Staines, Middlesex TW19 6AH. (Tel:0753-684633).
Electronic Publishing NOW: DZ Publishing Ltd., Aztec House, Vulcan Way, New Addington, CR0 9UG.(Tel: 0698 48521).
The Seybold Report on Desktop Publishing: Seybold Publications, Inc., PO Box 664, Media, PA 19063. (Tel: 215-565 2480).
The Wordsmith: The Old House, Church Rd., Kennington, Ashford, Kent TN24 9DQ. (Tel: 0233-39776).

DESKTOP PUBLISHING TRAINING
Together with **Alfred Marks Office Systems**, seminars and training are organised by **CCA Micro Rentals Ltd.**, Unit 7/8, Imperial Studios, Imperial Rd., London SW6 2AG. (Tel: 01-731 4310).

PUBLISHERS, MANUFACTURERS & DISTRIBUTORS
AB Designs, 81 Sutton Common Rd., Sutton, Surrey. (Tel: 01-664 6643).
Abacus Software, PO Box 7219, Grand Rapids, MI 49510, USA.
Acornsoft, Cambridge Technopark, 645 Newmarket Rd., Cambridge CB5 8PDE.
Addison-Wesley Ltd., Finchampstead Rd., Wokingham, Berks, RG11 2NZ. (Tel: 0734-794000).
Advanced Memory Systems, 166-170 Wilderspool Causeway, Warrington, WA4 6QA.

Aldus (UK) Ltd., Craigcrook Castle, Craigcrook Rd., Edinburgh EH4 3UH.
Alpha Software Corp, 30 B St., Burlington, MA 01803, USA. (Tel: 617 229 2924).
Anakin Research Inc., 100 Westmore Dr., Unit 11C, Rexdale, Ontario, Canada MV9 5C3. (Tel: 416 744-4246).
Apple Computer (UK) Ltd, Eastman Way, Hemel Hempstead, Herts, HP2 7HQ. (Tel: 0442-60244).
Applied Technology Marketing, CADCAM Centre, Middlesbrough, TS2 1RJ. (Tel: 0642 225854).

Appendix C

Appropriate Technology Ltd, Aptec House, South Bank Business Centre, Ponton Rd., London SW8 5AT. (Tel: 01–627 1000).

Apricot Computers plc, Apricot House, 111 Hagley Rd., Edgbaston, Birmingham B16 8LB.(Tel: 021–456 1234).

Ariolasoft Ltd., 68 Long Acre, London WC2E 9JH. (Tel: 01–836 3411).

ARS Microsystems, Doman Rd., Camberley, Surrey GU15 3DF. (Tel: 0276 685005).

Artsci Inc., 5547 Satsuma Avenue, North Hollywood, CA 91601, USA. (Tel: 818 985 2922).

AST Europe Ltd., AST House, 2 Goat Wharf, Brentford, Middlesex TW8 0BA. (Tel: 01–568 4600).

Autodesk Ltd., South Bank Technopark, 90 London Rd., London SE1 6LN. (Tel: 01–928 7868).

Beebugsoft, PO Box 109, High Wycombe, Bucks. (Tel: 0727–60263).

Bestinfo, 33 Chester Pike, Ridley Park, PA 19078, USA. (Tel: 215–521 0757).

Boston Publishing Systems, 1260 Boylston St., Boston, MA 02215, USA. (Tel: 617–267 4747).

Brown–Wagh Publishing, 16795 Lark Ave., Suite 210, Los Gatos, CA 95030, USA. (Tel: 1–800 451 0900).

C Ltd., 723 East Skinner, Wichita, KS 67211, USA. (Tel: 316–267 6321).

Canon (UK) Ltd., Canon House, Manor Rd., Wallington, Surrey SM6 0AJ. (Tel: 01–773 3173).

Cherry Electrical Products Ltd., Coldharbour Lane, Harpenden, Herts AL5 4UN. (Tel: 05827–63100).

CJE Micro's, 78 Brighton Rd., Worthing, W. Sussex BN11 2EN. (Tel: 0903 213361).

Clares, 98 Middlewich Rd., Northwich, Cheshire CW9 7DA. (Tel: 0606 48511).

Cognita, 34 Mallord St., London SW3 6DU. (Tel: 01–736 3637).

Computer Concepts, Gaddesdon Place, Hemel Hempstead, Herts HP2 6EX. (Tel: 0442–63933).

Computers Unlimited, 246 Regent's Park Rd., London N3 3HP (Tel: 01–349 2395).

CRL Group plc, CRL House, 9 Kings Yard, Carpenters Rd., London E15 2HD.

Ctrl Alt Del, 44 Brownbaker Court, Neath Hill, Milton Keynes, Bucks MK14 6JH. (Tel: 0908–662759).

DAK Industries Inc., 8200 Remmet Ave., Canoga Park, CA 91304, USA. (Tel: 1–800–423–2866).

Dart Electronics, Unit B5, Oulton Works, School Rd., Lowestoft, Suffolk NR33 9NA. (Tel: 0502–513707).

Database Software, Europa House, 68 Chester Rd., Hazel Grove, Stockport SK7 5NY. (Tel: 061–429 8008).

Datafood Software Company, 400 Country Drive, Suite H, Dover, DEL 19901, USA. (Tel: 302 736 9098).

Decisionware Inc., 2033 Wood St., Suite 218, Saratoga, Florida 33577, USA. (Tel: 813 9211).

Design Dynamics, 8 Meadow Way, Ampthill, Bedford MK45 2QX.

Digita, Kelsey House, Barns Rd., Budleigh Salterton, Devon EX9 6HJ. (Tel: 03954–5059).

Digital Precision, 222 The Avenue, London E4 9SE. (Tel: 01–527 5493).

Digital Research (UK) Ltd., Oxford House, Oxford St., Newbury, Berks RG13 1JB. (Tel: 0635 38787).

Digithurst Ltd., Church Lane, Royston, Herts SG8 9LG. (Tel: 0763–42955).

DOS (Europe) Ltd., PO Box 6, Brecon, Powysw, LD3 7YP. (Tel: 0874–5097).

Dynamic Graphics (UK) Ltd., Media House, Eastways Industrial Park, Witham, Essex CM8 3YJ. (Tel: 0376–516006).

Earthbound Software, Suite #237, 1005 E. 60th St., Chicago, IL 60637, USA. (Tel: 312–667 8048).

Eidersoft Software Ltd., The Office, Hall Farm, N. Ockendon, Upminster, Essex RM14 3QH. (Tel: 0708–856468).

Electric Software, Cromwell Business Centre, New Rd., St. Ives, Cambs PE17 4BG. (Tel: 0480–66433).

The Electric Studio, Unit 13, The Business Centre, Avenue One, Letchworth, Herts SG6 2HB. (Tel: 0462–675666).

Electronic Arts, 1820 Gateway Drive, San Mateo, CA 94404, USA. (Tel: 415 571 7171).

Esselte Letraset Ltd., St. George's House, 195–203 Waterloo Rd., London SE1 8XJ. (Tel: 01–928 7551).

ETAP, Steenovenstraat 1A, 2150 Malle, Belgium. (Tel 31–310 04 11).

First Analytical Ltd., 70 Borough High St., London SE1 1XF. (Tel: 01–430 5493).

Forest Marketing, 19 Hardingham St., Hingham, Norwich, Norfolk NR9 4JB. (Tel: 0603–667021).

Formscan Ltd., Apex House, West End, Frome, Somerset BA11 3AS. (Tel: 0373–61446).

FTL Systems Inc., 234 Eglinton Ave. East, Suite 205, Toronto, Ontario, Canada M4P 1K5. (Tel: 416–487 2142).

GAP Software, 17 St. John's Terrace, London E7 8BX.(Tel: 01–2 5452).

GB Techniques, Barclays Venture Centre, University of Warwick Science Park, Coventry, Worcs. CV4 7EZ. (Tel: 0203–413884).

Glentop Press Ltd., Standfast House, Bath Place, Barnet, Herts EN5 5XE. (Tel: 01–441 4130).

Gold Disk Software, PO Box 789, Streetsville, Ontario, L5M 2C2, Canada. (Tel: 1–416 828 0913).

Goldstein Software, 2 Redgate Ct., Silver Spring, MD 20904, USA. (Tel: 301–384 5565).

Grafsales Ltd., Unit Q2, Penfold Works, Imperial Way, Watford, Herts WD2 4YY. (Tel: 0923–43942).

HB Marketing Ltd., Pier Rd., North Feltham Trading Estate, Feltham, Middlesex TW14 0TT. (Tel: 01–751 6451).

Heyden & Son Ltd., Spectrum House, Hillview Gardens, London NW4 2JQ. (Tel: 01–203 5171).

Hisoft, 180 High St. North, Dunstable, Beds LU6 1AT. (Tel: 0582 696421).

Icon Technology, 9 Jarrom St., Leicester LE22 7DH. (Tel: 01–203 5171).

Ideal Software Ltd., Tolworth Tower, Surbiton, Surrey KT6 7EL. (Tel: 01–390 6722).

IHS Systems, 4178 Meridian Ave., Suite 211, San Jose, CA 95118, USA. (Tel: 408–265 5503).

Infinity, 1144 65th Street, Suite C, Emeryville, CA 94608, USA. (Tel: 415–420–1551).

I/O Video, 222 Third St., Cambridge, MA 012 42, USA. (Tel: 617–547 4141).

Kenilworth Computers Ltd., 19 Talisman Square, Kenilworth, Warwickshire CV8 1JB. (Tel: 0926 512127).

Koala Technologies, 3100 Patrick Henry Dr., Santa Clara, CA 95052, USA. (Tel: 408–986 8866).

Kuma, 12 Horseshoe Park, Pangbourne, Berks RG8 7JW. (Tel: 07357–4335).

Kurta Corp., 4610 S. 35th St., Phoenix AZ 85040, USA. (Tel: 602 276 5533).

Lasermaker, Advertiser House, Long Eaton, Notts. (Tel: 0602–731803).

Lexisoft Inc., PO Box 1950, Davis, CA 95617, USA. (Tel: 916–758 9233).

Linear Graphics Ltd., 28 Purdeys Way, Rochford, Essex, SS4 1NE. (Tel: 0702–541663).

Lotus Development (UK) Ltd., Consort House, Victoria St., Windsor, Berks SL4 1EX. (Tel: 0734–342875).

MacEurope Ltd., 9a Lyne Court, Church Lane, London NW9. (Tel: 01–200 3981).

McQueen Ltd., Elliot House, 8–10 Hillside Crescent, Edinburgh EH7 5EA. (Tel: 031–558 3333).

MacSerious Company, 17 Park Circus Place, Glasgow G3 6AH. (Tel: 041–332 5622).

MacSoft, Bridge House, Wellington, Somerset TA21 0AA. (Tel: 082–347 3625).

Management Graphics Inc, 1450 Lodestar Rd., Unit No 1, Downsview, Ontario, Canada. (Tel: 416–638 8877).

Mayfield UK Ltd., 96, R. Walton Rd., Moleseley, Surrey. (Tel: 01–941–6066).

Microillusions, PO Box 3475, Granada Hills, CA 91344, USA. (Tel: 8181–360 3715).

MicroSearch Inc., 9896 Southwest Freeway, Houston, Texas 77074, USA. (Tel: 713–988 2818).

Microsoft UK, Excel House, 49 De Montfort Rd., Reading, Berks. (Tel: 0734–500741).

Microspot, London House, 5–11 London Rd., Maidstone, Kent ME16 8HR. (Tel: 0622–687771).

Micro Studio, 83 Clay St., Soham, Cambs CB7 5HL.

Mirrorsoft, Maxwell House, 74 Worship St., London EC2A 2EN. (Tel: 01–377 4645).

John Morrison, 4 Rein Gardens, Tingley, W. Yorkshire WF3 1JR. (Tel: 0532–537 507).

New Horizons Software, PO Box 43167, Austin, Texas 7845, USA. (Tel: 512–280 0319).

Newtek Ltd., &01 Jackson, Suite B3, Topeka, Kansas, USA. (Tel: 913–354 9332).

The Other Guys, 55 North Main St., Suite 301–D, PO Box H, Logan, UT 84321, USA. (Tel: 801–735 7620).

P & P Micro Distributors Ltd., Todd Hall Rd., Carrs Industrial Estate, Haslingden, Rossendale, Lancs BB4 5HU. (Tel: 0706 217744).

Personal TEX Inc, 12 Madrona Ave., Mill Valley, CA 94941, USA. (Tel: 415–388 8853).

Pineapple Software, 39 Brownlea Gardens, Seven Kings, Ilford, Essex 1G3 9NL. (Tel: 01–599 1476).

Polaroid UK Ltd., Ashley Rd., St. Albans, Herts AL1 5PR. (Tel: 0727–59191).

PMS, 38 Cameron Drive, St. Leonards, East Kilbride. (Tel: 03552–32796).

Precision Software Ltd, 6 Park Terrace, Worcester Park, Surrey (Tel: 01–330 7166).

Pride Utilities, 7 Chalton Heights, Chalton, Luton, Beds LU4 9UF. (Tel: 0582–411686).

Python Microsystems, Unit 9, The Maltings, High St., Burwell, Cambridgeshire CB5 0HB. (Tel: 0638–741866).

Rainbird Software, Wellington House, Upper St. Martins Lane, London WC2H 9DL. (Tel: 01–240 8838).

Rank Xerox UK, Bridge House, Oxford Rd., Uxbridge, Middlesex UB8 1HS. (Tel: 0895–51133).

Raven Computers, 28–32 Cheapside, Bradford, W. Yorks. (Tel: 0274–309386).

Rombo Productions, 107 Raeburn Rigg, Knightsbridge, Livingstone, West Lothian EH54 8PH. (Tel: 0506–39046).

Samna International Ltd., Southbank House, Black Prince Rd., SE1 7JS.

S. Anthony Studios, 889 De Haro St., San Francisco, CA 94107, USA. (Tel: 415 826 6193).

Scenic Computer Systems Corp., 14852 NE 31st Circle, Redmond, WA 98052, USA. (Tel: 206–885 5500).

Sentinel Software Ltd., Wellington House, New Zealand Avenue, Walton on Thames, Surrey KT12 1P4. (Tel: 0932–231164).

Serif Software Ltd., 34 Landsdowne Crescent, Glasgow, G20 6NJ. (Tel: 041 339 2655).

Sherston Software, 8 Court St., Sherston, Malmesbury, Wilts SN16 0LL. (Tel: 0666 840433).

Silica Shop Ltd., 1–4 The Mews, Hatherley Rd., Sidcup, Kent DA14 4DX. (Tel: 01–309 1111).

Siren Technology, Trafford Technology Centre, 43 Elsinore Rd., Manchester M16 0WG. (Tel: 061–848 9233).

SoftCraft Inc., 222 State St, #400 Madison, WI 53703, USA. (Tel: 608–257 3300).

SoftStyle Inc., 7192 Kalanianaole Hwy, #205 Honolulu, HI 96825, USA.

Software City, St Andrews House, 22–28 High St., Epson, Surrey KT19 8AH.

Software Publishing Europe, 85–87 Jermyn St., London SW1Y 6JD. (Tel: 01–839 2840).

Spies Laboratories, PO Box 336, Lawndale, CA 90260, USA. (Tel: 213–538 8166).

SSI Ltd., Wellington House, New Zealand Avenue, Walton-on–Thames, Surrey, KT12 1PY. (Tel: 0932–231164).

Studio Software, 17862–C Fitch, Irvine, CA 92714, USA.

Summagraphics Ltd., 3/4 Winchcombe Rd., Newbury, Berks RG14 5QY. (Tel: 0635–32257).

Tasman Software, Springfield House, Hyde Terrace, Leeds LS2 9LN. (Tel: 0532–438301).

Technomatic, 305 Edgeware Rd., London W2. (Tel:01–723 0233).

Thames Valley Systems, Greys House, 7 Greyfriars Rd., Reading RG1 1NU. (Tel: 0734–581829)

Thunderware Inc., 19G Orinda Way,

Timatic Systems, The Market, Fareham, Hampshire. (Tel: 0329–236727).

TK Computerware, Stone St., North Stanford, Ashford, Kent CT25 6DF. (Tel: 0303–81 2801).

T/Maker Company, 1973 Landings Drive, Mt. View, CA 94043, USA. (Tel: 415–962 0195).

Unified Technology, 8 Canal Street, Manchester M1 3HE. (Tel: 061–236 8406).

Viza Software, Florence House, 54 High St., Maidstone, Kent. (Tel: 0634–45002).

Watford Electronics, Jessa House, 250 Lower High St., Watford WD1 2AN. (Tel: 0923–37774).

Wight Scientific, 44 Roan St., London SE10 9JT. (Tel: 01–858 2699).

Wordcraft International Ltd., Cowdray Centre House, Cowdray Avenue, Colchester, Essex CO1 1GH. (Tel:0206–561608).

Writing Consultants, 11 Creekbend Dr., Fairport, NY 14450, USA. (Tel:716–377 0130).

Wyse Technology (UK) Ltd., 26–28 King St., Maidenhead, Berks SL6 1EF. (Tel:0628–784037).

XLent Software (UK), 516 Alum Rock Rd., Alum Rock, Birmingham, B8 3HX. (Tel:021–327 6110).

Xyquest, 3 Loomis St., Bedford, MA 01730, USA. (Tel:617–275 4439).

ZSoft Corpn., 1950 Spectrum Circle, Suite A495, Marietta, GA 30067, USA.

Index

Index